THE STAFFORDSHIRE CAKES AND ALE TRAIL

First published in Great Britain by Pierrepoint Press 2012

Copyright © Bob Bibby

Bob Bibby has asserted his right under the Copyright, Designs and Patents Act 1988 to be identified as the author of this book.

A CIP record for this book is available from the British Library.

ISBN 978 0 9533196-8-8

All rights reserved. No part of this publication may be reproduced, stored in a retrieval system, or transmitted, in any form or by any means, electronic, mechanical, photocopying, recording or otherwise, without the prior permission of the publisher, nor be otherwise circulated in any form of binding or cover other than that in which it is published and without a similar condition including this condition being imposed on the subsequent purchaser.

Cover design by Clare Brayshaw

Typeset, printed and bound in Great Britain by:

York Publishing Services Ltd
64 Hallfield Road
Layerthorpe
York
YO31 7ZQ
Tel: 01904 431213

Website: www.yps-publishing.co.uk

THE STAFFORDSHIRE CAKES AND ALE TRAIL

Bob Bibby

Published by Pierrepoint Press

Other books by Bob Bibby

Travel Writing

Grey Paes and Bacon: From the Heart of the Black Country

Dancing with Sabrina: The River Severn –
a Journey from Source to Sea

Special Offa: A Walk along Offa's Dyke

On the Wall with Hadrian

Travel Writing

The Shropshire Cakes and Ale Trail

The Worcestershire Cakes and Ale Trail

The Warwickshire Cakes and Ale Trail

Crime Fiction

Be a Falling Leaf

Bird on the Wing

The Liquidator

The Llareggub Experience

Fiction

Known Unto God

www.bobbibby.co.uk

To Enid

Acknowledgements

Thanks for the use of particular images to:

Nick Catford & Subterranea Britannica for Swynnerton Training Area, to Kevin Gallagher for the Tutbury Jinny, to The History Press for the cover of *Cartimandua, Queen of the Brigantes*, and to Peter Jones for Eccleshall Castle tower.

All other images by Bob & Enid Bibby.

Special thanks to Dr Trevor James for an early reading of the text and extra information about Staffordshire and to John Rowe for testing the route out with me.

"Dost thou think, because thou art virtuous, there shall be no more cakes and ale?"

Sir Toby Belch in *Twelfth Night*

CONTENTS

INTRODUCTION

Origins of the Trail	viii
Planning the Walk	x
Ordnance Survey Maps	x
Explanatory Notes	xi

ROUTE

1. Burton-upon-Trent to Lichfield	1
2. Lichfield to Penkridge	13
3. Penkridge to Eccleshall	29
4. Eccleshall to Stone	41
5. Stone to Cheadle	55
6. Cheadle to Uttoxeter	67
7. Uttoxeter to Burton-upon-Trent	83

USEFUL INFORMATION

Tourist Information Centres	97
Other Contacts	97
Useful Websites	97
Suggested Reading	98
Distance Checklist	99

INTRODUCTION

Origins of the Trail

This is the fourth in my series of County Cakes and Ale Trails. Inspired by the success of *The Shropshire Cakes and Ale Trail*, *The Worcestershire Cakes and Ale Trail* and *The Warwickshire Cakes and Ale Trail*, I decided to set about creating a similar long-distance walk in the neighbouring county of Staffordshire. The idea, as previously, was to build a seven-day circular walk, averaging about fifteen miles a day, linking up some of the small towns and ensuring a good pub for lunchtime ale, a good café for afternoon cakes and a choice of pubs for evening ales.

Staffordshire calls itself "the creative county", largely because of the work begun by Josiah Wedgwood that led to the creation of The Potteries in the Stoke-on-Trent area. However, it can also boast other significant creators – Robert Peel, whose brain-child was the police force, was MP for Tamworth, Joseph Bamford developed the huge JCB empire, Dr Samuel Johnson produced the great English dictionary, and William Bass created one of the largest beer brewing industries in the United Kingdom. So it's no surprise to find that many pubs in the county boast of the quality of their food and beer and that there are a number of small breweries, such as Burton Bridge, Slater's and Titanic producing high-quality Real Ales that you may come across on the route, as well as the ubiquitous Marston's, still brewed in Burton-upon-Trent itself.

In *The Shropshire Cakes and Ale Trail* I summoned Sir Toby Belch's anguished protest at the restrictions which Malvolio, that arch Puritan, was seeking to impose on Toby and his merry friends:

"Dost thou think, because thou art virtuous, there shall be no more cakes and ale?"

to support my argument for creating a walk that uses beer and pubs as central to its purpose. Sir Toby's cry echoes down the centuries against all those who would restrict the pleasures of life, who want us to drink only water and eat only salads, and whose idea of exercise is walking on a treadmill in a gym with a heart monitor attached to you.

So *The Staffordshire Cakes and Ale Trail* also aims to respond to the doom and gloom so prevalent in modern life, as well as providing a real opportunity for those who enjoy walking to step it out beside the Staffordshire canals, up its hills and along its dales and at the same time to enjoy some of the Real Ales in some of Staffordshire's great pubs. So, although this walk is intended as a seven-day challenge, it should also be attempted with an open mind and a cheerful spirit.

Staffordshire, like most counties nowadays, is criss-crossed by a number of other long-distance paths, some of whose routes in places coincide with mine and each of which has its own attractions. The Staffordshire Way, the Heart of England Way and The Way for the Millennium all coincide at times with my route. Many of these paths I have walked but none fulfilled all that I wanted, particularly in terms of offering good accommodation, good pubs and good cafés. That is why I have created my own route. Staffordshire has a varied landscape, so *The Staffordshire Cakes and Ale Trail* includes stretches beside the canals that opened up the county to trade, routes through the National Forest, an Area of Outstanding Natural Beauty on Cannock Chase and over the hilly territory of the Staffordshire Moorlands in the north, following public rights of way or, occasionally, minor roads.

Staffordshire is threaded with a large number of well-signposted footpaths that take the observant walker through ancient woodlands, past the haunts of birds and mammals, over rolling countryside, and beside the fast-flowing waters of the River Churnet and the River Dove. The best views on *The Staffordshire Cakes and Ale Trail* are from the Castle Ring on Cannock Chase, from the toposcope just outside Swynnerton, from Toot Hill near Alton and from around Hanbury but there are other pleasing vistas throughout the journey.

The towns which I have used as the base points for each section of *The Staffordshire Cakes and Ale Trail* – Burton-upon-Avon, Lichfield, Penkridge, Eccleshall, Stone, Cheadle and Uttoxeter – all have their own intriguing histories and secrets, as well as providing plenty of opportunities for walkers to take rest in a range of accommodation, take cake in the cafés and take ale in the characterful pubs and hotels. The route also leads walkers through or past many other places of interest – Norman churches and the glorious Lichfield Cathedral, stately homes, archaeological sites, historical ruins, wonderful castles, Iron Age hillforts, and other more modern curiosities – as well as introducing them to some of the colourful characters who have contributed to the spirit of the county.

Although I have begun and ended my route in Burton-upon-Trent, walkers may wish to find their own point of entry. Likewise, although the route is described in seven sections, each of which is approximately 15 miles long, walkers who do not have the opportunity to follow the route for seven consecutive days or who do not have the energy to cover these distances will find their own ways of managing. My hope is that any who follow in my footsteps will experience as much pleasure as I did in walking *The Staffordshire Cakes and Ale Trail*.

Planning the Walk

Those used to long days of walking on a regular basis should have no problems in covering *The Staffordshire Cakes and Ale Trail*. A reasonable amount of stamina and fitness should sustain such walkers on the journey (as will the cakes and ale!). Be aware, however, that there is a difference between a good Sunday walk and walking fifteen miles every day for a week. Getting good miles under your feet in preparation will pay off in terms of your enjoyment and comfort during your journey.

As regards equipment and clothing, I prefer to travel as light as possible but it is essential to have a good waterproof jacket and trousers. Boots (well worn in, of course) are necessary too, since the terrain in places can be quite demanding and ankles need support. If journeying in hot weather, you may be tempted to wear shorts but be prepared that at such times and in some places paths can become overgrown with nettles and/or brambles, so keep your overtrousers handy. A walking pole is a useful accessory for warding off such vegetation, as well as for shooing away inquisitive cows. Be aware also that some parts of the trail, especially where it coincides with a bridleway, can be very muddy. If arranging accommodation in advance, you might consider posting changes of clothing, new maps etc to and from where you are staying.

The walk can be done at any time of the year, though potential walkers need to beware of the River Dove flooding south of Uttoxeter. The best period is probably late spring when you are likely to enjoy the fabulous blossom of the countryside at its brightest but it is an equally-pleasant experience from May to October.

Ordnance Survey Maps

The following Ordnance Survey 1:25000 maps are essential for following the route. Each has been referenced in the appropriate section.

Explorer 245: The National Forest

Explorer 244: Cannock Chase & Chasewater

Explorer 242: Telford, Ironbridge & The Wrekin

Explorer 243: Market Drayton

Explorer 258: Stoke-on-Trent & Newcastle-under-Lyme

Explorer 259: Derby

Explanatory Notes

The Staffordshire Cakes and Ale Trail guide to the walk itself is set out in seven sections, each with its own introduction which includes a gradient summary, a brief description of the terrain for that section and a mileage chart. Each section is then further subdivided into subsections of varying distances which have a narrative and diagrams of the route on one page with photographs and text about features encountered during the walk on the opposite page. The diagrams are NOT to scale but are intended to indicate the direction of the trail, particularly at junctions of paths and/or roads. The diagrams should be used in combination with the relevant Ordnance Survey Explorer Map.

Each section concludes with photographs of the town where that day's walking finishes, together with a brief history of the place and an account of some of the celebrities whose names linger there. Finally, and this book would be pointless without it, there is a guide to some of the cafés and pubs in that town, together with an accommodation list and other essential information about facilities (Post Office, bank ATMs, Tourist Information Centre, Transport connections) in each. Naturally, other walkers may find different cafés and different pubs to the ones I have indicated. The selection is entirely my own and therefore entirely idiosyncratic. The accommodation list is not a recommended list but merely an indication of possibilities. Be aware, of course, that changes do occur and these listings will not be accurate for ever.

Countryside Code

- Be safe – plan ahead and follow any signs
- Leave gates and property as you find them
- Protect plants and animals, and take your litter home
- Keep dogs under close control
- Consider other people

ADVICE TO READERS
You are advised that, although every effort has been made to ensure the accuracy of this guidebook, changes may occur. It is sensible to check in advance on transport and accommodation but rights of way can also sometimes be amended.

CHEADLE

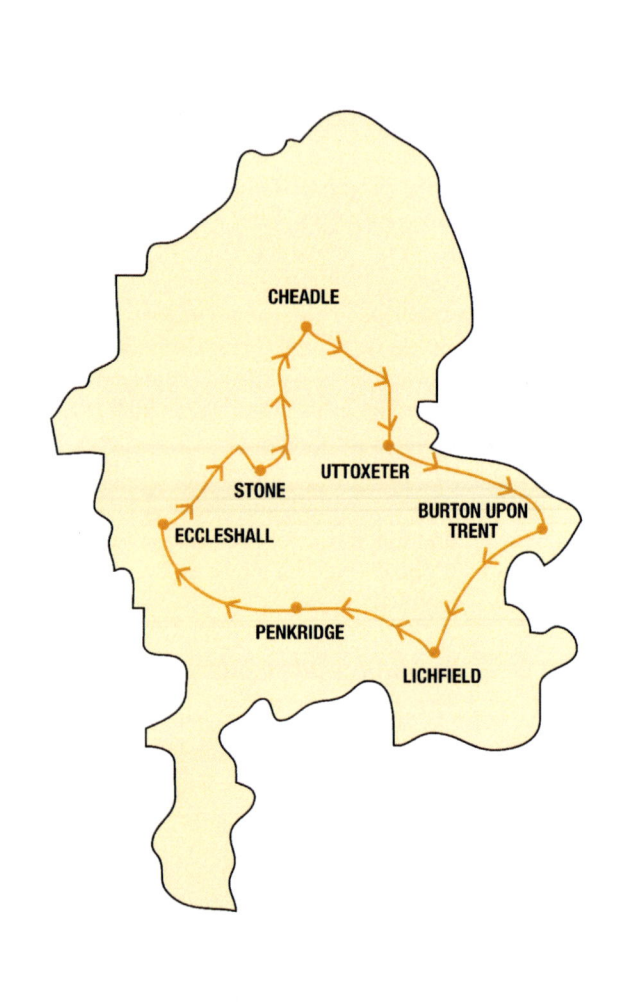

UTTOXETER

STONE

ECCLESHALL

BURTON UPON TRENT

PENKRIDGE

LICHFIELD

BURTON-UPON-TRENT – LICHFIELD

OS Map: Explorer 245

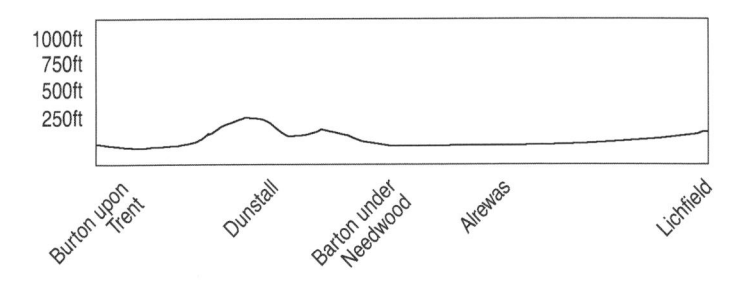

This day's walk begins with an easy stretch out of Burton-upon-Trent along the towpath of the Trent & Mersey Canal, before branching across country and on to the slight rise that houses the magnificent Dunstall Hall and the village church of St Mary. Next it's across fields and through woodland to reach the ancient village of Barton-under-Needwood in the heart of the National Forest. From there a pleasant green lane takes you to rejoin the Trent & Mersey Canal leading into the village of Alrewas for a mid-journey break at The Crown and a possible detour to the National Memorial Arboretum.

The final section of the day's walk again takes you along the canal towpath past Fradley Junction, once an important intersection on the canal network. You leave the canal as it turns north and go south along the Curborough Brook, past a motor car sprint course, and that brings you into the city of Lichfield with its magnificent three-spired cathedral, visible for many miles.

PLACE	DAILY MILES	TOTAL MILES
Burton-upon-Trent	-	-
Dunstall	4.5	4.5
Alrewas	8.5	8.5
Fradley Junction	10.5	10.5
Lichfield	13.5	13.5

BURTON-UPON-TRENT to LICHFIELD
(13.5 miles)

Burton-upon-Trent to Dunstall (4.5 miles)

- Outside railway station go left, then left again on Curzon Street. Follow to join Wellington Street. Go left and 100 yards before traffic island go right through alleyway on to The Grange. At end of street, go left on Grange Street, and then at T-junction go right on Shobnall Road.
- Go past Shobnall Marina and descend left on to towpath of Trent & Mersey Canal, passing underneath Marston's Pedigree sign, with Marston's Brewery to right.
- Continue on towpath for some distance to reach Tatenhill Lock by Bridge 35 in Branston Water Park. Go right over bridge and take footpath signposted Tatenhill between pools.
- Leave Water Park via gate and, after 300 yards, go left over stile opposite footbridge. Go diagonally right across field to metal gate.
- Go right on broad track for 200 yards then go left over plank bridge in hedge. (N.B. path has changed around here). Follow path around perimeter of sand and gravel extraction pits to metal gate by road.
- Just before gate, go left over plank bridge and follow right field boundary over further plank bridge and stile to reach stile on to road at T-junction by signpost for Dunstall.
- Cross road and go over stile to take footpath across field to further stile. Go left on road into Dunstall, passing Dunstall Hall on left and St Mary's church on right.

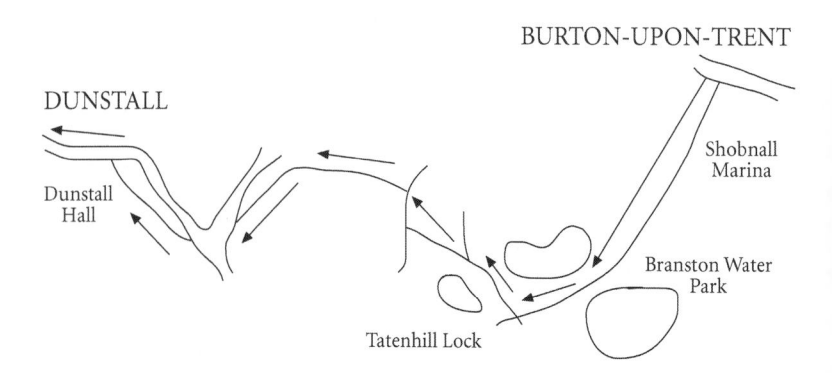

BRANSTON

Branston is best known for the pickle that bears its name and used to be made there in a factory that began life as the National Machine Gun Factory, although production has now shifted to Bury St Edmunds. Branston Pickle, made inevitably to a secret recipe, is a mixture of diced vegetables and a sweetly-sticky sauce; it is popular with cheese in sandwiches as part of a Ploughman's Lunch, though ploughmen never knew about it.

What was once the separate village of Branston, at one time owned by the infamous Lady Godiva, is now little more than an extension of Burton-upon-Trent along the A38. Within its bounds is Sinai Park Farm, which used to be a sanatorium for sick monks from Burton Abbey. Adjoining the Trent & Mersey Canal is Branston Water Park, formed in what had once been a quarry. This forty-acre site includes extensive woodland and parkland, while the Water Park is popular with anglers, birdwatchers and windsurfers.

DUNSTALL

Dunstall is a tiny attractive village of few houses, two or three farms, a church and the estate of the stately home known as Dunstall Hall. It also houses a practical joke, for anyone ever asked to go for a drink at the White Lion finds themselves not in a pub but at the water fountain placed in the village for Queen Victoria's Jubilee. Ho, ho!

Dunstall Hall was originally a lodge on the edge of the Royal Forest of Needwood, bought with its estate by the son of the spinning jenny inventor Richard Arkwright for his son Charles. Between 1856 and 1890 significant alterations were carried out to produce the Hall that is seen today. At the entrance to the Hall stands an 1850's Ionic porte-cochère. The parapet is fretted to form "IS QUI DEDIT MIHI SERVET" (He who has given watches over me), dating from 1652 and removed from the old Hall. In 2007 the Hall was opened as a venue for weddings, business meetings and conferences for those who have nothing better to do with their money (or want to know what a porte-cochère is).

Dunstall to Alrewas (4 miles)

- Just after church go left on footpath and, just before No Access sign by Smith Hills Cottages, go left again through gate and take bridleway climbing diagonally left across field to enter woodland by gate
- Go ahead through two further gates on to clear descending path across long field to gate then stile. Continue through further gate to emerge by Village Hall in Barton-under-Needwood opposite Middle Bell pub.
- Go left on road through village. At St James's church go right on first footpath beside church and reach road. Go right for 30 yards then through metal barriers to pass children's play area. Take right-forking path through narrow walkway to reach Wales Lane.
- Go left on road for some way to reach Royal Oak. Go left on Dogshead Lane and after 300 yards go right on footpath signposted Wychnor.
- Continue on wide track through fields to reach T-junction. Go straight ahead towards St Leonard's church in Wychnor.
- Just before church go through gate on right and descend through field to rejoin towpath of canal.
- Go right and follow towpath to Bridge 46. Go up on to Church Road, turn left and then right into Post Office Road to The Crown (01283-790328) in Alrewas.

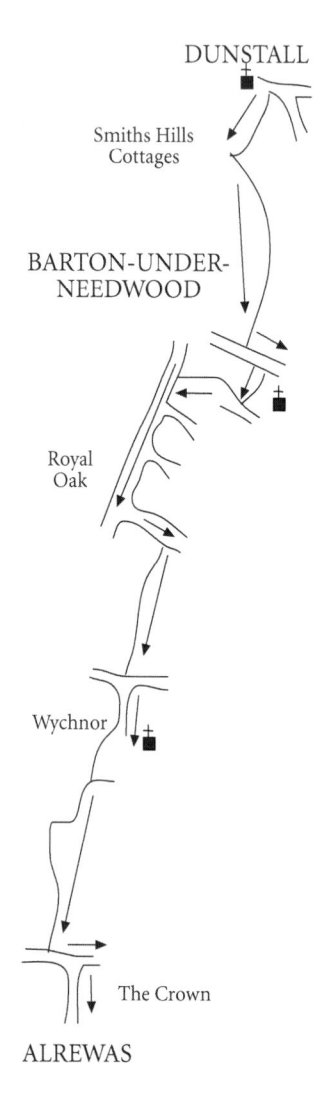

BARTON-UNDER-NEEDWOOD

Barton-under-Needwood was originally a Saxon settlement but its story really centres around its church of St James, originally built between 1517 and 1533 under the auspices of John Taylor. He was the eldest of triplet boys presented to Henry VII who came to hunt in the forest of Needwood and met the boys' father, a forest game warden. King Henry saw in them a sign of the Holy Trinity and promised to educate them if they grew to manhood. All survived and became Doctors of Canon Law. John became one of the King's Chaplains, Archdeacon of Derby and Buckingham, Master of the Rolls and an international diplomat, who attended Henry VIII when he met Francis I of France on the Field of the Cloth of Gold in 1520.

Barton-under-Needwood is now a commuter village of some 5000 residents with several pubs, a marina for boats, a number of older houses and a high school, inevitably named after John Taylor.

ALREWAS

Alrewas is a large village that sits at the junction of Rykneild Street (A38) and the salt route from Cheshire to Lincoln and at the intersection of the River Trent with the Trent & Mersey Canal. It is an old settlement, once owned by Earl Leofric of Mercia and, after the Norman conquest, by the crown until the time of King John. The main street contains many black-and-white thatched cottages, many of them dating from the 16th century.

The National Memorial Arboretum situated to the east of the village contains memorials to all those who have died on duty or as a result of terrorist action since the Second World War, its most recent addition being the Basra Memorial Wall. The memorials are surrounded by 50,000 trees of different varieties, chosen for their relevance to one or more of the memorials.

The 600-year old Crown Inn is an old coaching inn in the centre of the village that serves a range of Real Ales, including Bass, Marston's and Hook Norton, plus good food and is CAMRA-recommended. It is a good mid-journey resting point.

Alrewas to Lichfield (5 miles)

- Retrace steps to Bridge 46 on Trent & Mersey Canal and go left through Alrewas village. Continue on towpath to pass Common Lock, Hunt's Lock and Keeper's Lock and reach busy Fradley Junction.
- At Shadehouse Lock, cross canal Bridge 52 and go over stile on right to take path on opposite side of canal. After 80 yards take right-forking path and continue on path parallel to canal. Where canal bends north, continue on path to reach road. Cross road and go diagonally right across field to gap between trees and fence,
- Continue ahead for 30 yards then join surfaced track bending to right of Curborough Sprint Course. After 100 yards go right over footbridge and follow path through woodland and alongside sewage works to stile.
- Over stile go straight ahead on line of telegraph poles, going left of farm buildings to reach gate on drive by Field House. Go immediately left through further gate and after 30 yards cross track and footbridge.
- Go right beside fishing pools. After second pool go straight ahead to stile and up to field. Go right along treeline and, where trees end, take left-forking path bending to run parallel with railway line. Go over two stiles beside road bend and continue to further stile. Go right over railway footbridge.
- Go straight ahead on cul-de-sac for 30 yards then go left on alleyway. Continue on road for 80 yards then go right on alleyway. Go right on next road and cross main road on to further alleyway. Go ahead to cross Netherstowe Road and take left path towards city centre.
- Cross next road and go straight ahead to path beside Stowe Pool into the Close. Go right for cathedral or left for Lichfield city centre.

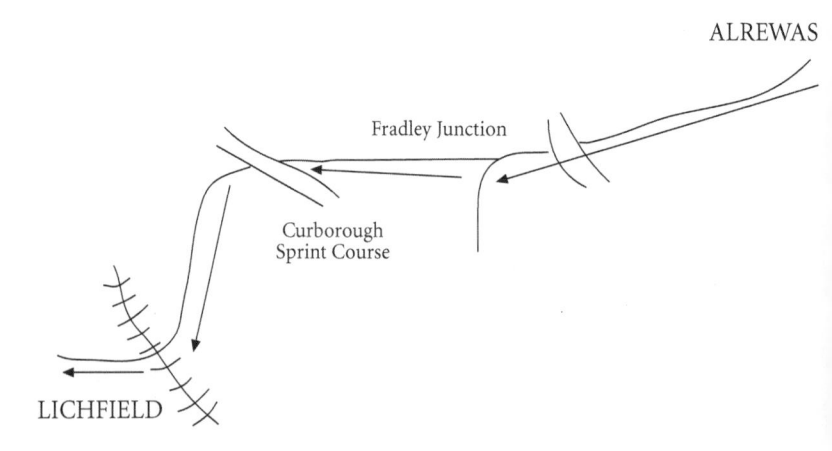

FRADLEY JUNCTION

Fradley was a major junction on the Victorian canal network, linking the Coventry Canal to the Trent & Mersey Canal in 1790. Both canal companies built houses for their workers at Fradley and two large warehouses, complete with hoists, were erected alongside The Swan public house. These are all now listed buildings.

British Waterways still has an office here and it is a popular stopping off place for boaters. There are two cafés and two shops as well as The Swan Inn to cater for boaters and gongoozlers*. There is also Fradley Pool Nature Reserve, which includes a board walk, a bird hide and pond-dipping platforms.

- *A gongoozler is a person addicted to watching canal life, a sort of canal anorak.*

CURBOROUGH SPRINT COURSE

The small sprint course was originally part of the RAF Lichfield base that was purchased by a local farmer in the early 1960s. The Shenstone & District Car Club secured a lease on the sprint course at that time and still use it under those arrangements. There have been a number of improvements over the years and the present short course is 900 yards, while the long course is 1557 yards. The current short course record, just in case you are interested, is 26.84 seconds and was achieved in 1996 by Roy Lane in a Pilbeam MP58-09. Fascinating, eh?

CURBOROUGH SPRINT COURSE

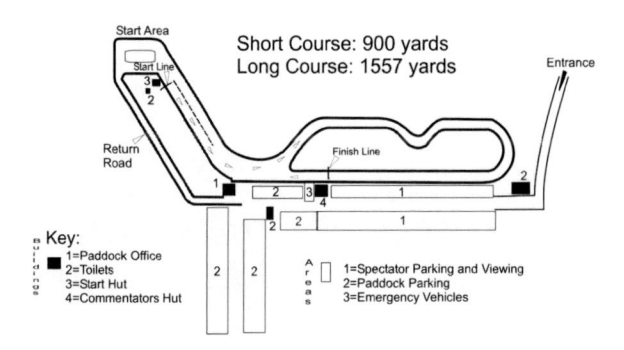

LICHFIELD PIX

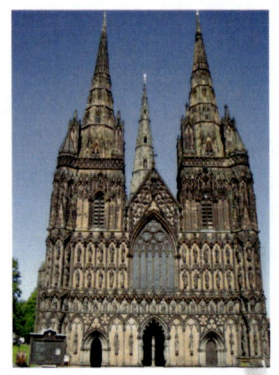

Lichfield Cathedral

Dr Johnson

Lichfield Garrick Theatre

Erasmus Darwin House

James Boswell

Samuel Johnson Birthplace Museum

LICHFIELD STORY

I lately took my friend Boswell and showed him genuine civilised life in an English provincial town.

Dr Samuel Johnson

Lichfield's origins lie in Roman times, although its significance as a city dates to 669 when the see was given to St Chad, Bishop of the Mercians, who established a ministry here that in 700 became the very first version of Lichfield Cathedral. Under King Offa the bishopric became an archbishopric, although this did not endure for long after Offa's death. The Cathedral was rebuilt and added to by the Anglo-Normans when its distinctive three spires were built. One of these spires collapsed during the Civil War when the city, a Royalist stronghold, was besieged and bombarded by the Parliamentarian troops. Subsequent rebuilding in the 17th and 19th centuries has left the present attractive building, visible from many miles around Lichfield and a famous tourist spot. Its treasures include the Anglo-Saxon Lichfield Bible, the recently-found Lichfield Angel and the Herkenrode Glass in the Lady Chapel.

The Cathedral has two pools adjacent to it – Minster Pool and Stowe Pool. Taken together with the elegant Georgian buildings of The Close that surrounds the Cathedral and of Dam Street that connects it to the city centre, these provide the pleasantest vista in Lichfield. In the 14th and 15th centuries, Lichfield was the largest town in Staffordshire and its prosperity grew with the coming of the coaching trade in the 18th century, when much rebuilding of the centre took place, leaving many of the appealing Georgian buildings still evident today.

Daniel Defoe called Lichfield an area where 'good conversation and good company' could be guaranteed and intellectual life flourished here. Its most famous son, Dr Johnson, brought his biographer James Boswell to visit the town and there are statues of both Johnson and Boswell in the market place, the former facing the house the great lexicographer grew up in – now the Samuel Johnson Birthplace Museum. As well as Johnson and his equally-famous pupil, the actor David Garrick, Erasmus Darwin, the grandfather of the evolutionist Charles Darwin, lived here and his house is also now open to visitors.

The coming of the railways and the canals in the 19th century passed Lichfield by and this probably saved the city centre as many of its fine old buildings have been preserved and can be seen in the centre, such as the Guildhall and the George Hotel. Since the 1950s there has been a massive expansion of the population when Lichfield provided overspill housing for many from the burgeoning West Midlands conurbation. It now has a fast train service to Birmingham.

LICHFIELD CELEBRITIES

Elias Ashmole (1617-1692)
In 1650 Elias Ashmole, son of a Lichfield saddler, met John Tradescant, who with his father had built a huge collection of exotic plants and curiosities. Ashmole helped Tradescant to catalogue this collection and persuaded him to leave everything to him in his will. On Tradescant's death his widow claimed that her husband had signed this will when he was drunk but the courts found in Ashmole's favour, allowing him to donate the whole collection to Oxford University. The Ashmolean, the first public museum in Europe, opened in 1683.

Samuel Johnson (1709-1784)
Dr Johnson is chiefly known nowadays for being the compiler of his own *Dictionary of the English Language* in 1755 and as the subject of James Boswell's *Life of Samuel Johnson*, published in 1791. Born above his father's bookshop in Lichfield, Johnson was educated in the town but was unable to complete his studies at Oxford because of debt. He wrote essays, poems, plays, criticism and biography, but devoted over ten years of his life to his dictionary. A major literary figure of his time, he was buried in Westminster Abbey.

David Garrick (1717-1779)
David Garrick was the leading actor of his time. He made his name initially playing Shakespeare's *Richard III*, following which he was invited to join the acting company at Drury Lane. He took over management of Drury Lane in 1747 and led it for twenty-nine years to become one of the greatest playhouses in Europe. His playing of the great Shakespearian roles made him enormously popular with audiences. He also initiated the Shakespeare Jubilee Festival in Stratford-upon-Avon in 1769. He too was buried in Westminster Abbey.

Erasmus Darwin (1731-1802)
Erasmus Darwin, grandfather of Charles, established his medical practice in Lichfield in his twenties where he formed the Lichfield Botanical Society to translate the works of Linnaeus into English. His writings greatly foreshadowed the theory of evolution but he was also an inventor of, among other things, a copying machine and a minute artificial bird. He opposed the slave trade, was in favour of the education of women, and supported the French and American Revolutions. He was a man far ahead of his time.

LICHFIELD CAKES

CHAPTERS, *The Close*
Old building with bags of atmosphere adjacent to cathedral. Offers range of sandwiches, homemade cakes and pastries plus selection of teas and coffees. Very pleasant, sheltered garden area.

COUCH POTATO CAFÉ, *55 Wade Street*
Very popular with big, comfy couches and newspapers. Friendly, relaxed atmosphere with first-rate friendly service.

HINDLEYS BAKERY, *10 Tamworth Street*
Bread baked on premises used to make high-quality sandwiches and toasties. Also offers wide range of homemade cakes, plus range of teas and coffees in its café.

THREE SPIRES, *10a Market Street*
Offers a range of sandwiches, paninis, cakes together with teas and range of speciality coffees (amoretto, hazelnut etc). Also offers free computer usage.

LICHFIELD ALE

DUKE OF WELLINGTON, *Birmingham Road*
Open plan but with three distinct drinking areas, and lawned garden, favourite with Real Ale fans, friendly atmosphere. Serves London Pride, Marston's, Adnam's, Abbot Ale, plus Thatcher's cider.

GEORGE & DRAGON, *Beacon Street*
Small two-room pub north of cathedral – lounge tells story of Siege of Lichfield. Serves Banks's & Marston's.

KING'S HEAD, *Bird Street*
Former coaching inn that claims to be the birthplace of Staffordshire Regiment and has military paraphernalia as decor. Serves Banks's & Marston's.

QUEEN'S HEAD, *Queen Street*
Elongated single-room pub, mecca for Real Ale lovers, serving Adnam's, Marston's, Timothy Taylor & Batham's. Known for good quality, reasonably-priced food.

LICHFIELD ACCOMMODATION

32 Beacon Street, Lichfield, WS13 7AJ (Tel:01543-262378)

Altair House, 21 Shakespeare Avenue, Lichfield, WS14 9BE
(Tel: 01543-252900)

Bogey Hole, 21-23 Dam Street, Lichfield, WS13 6AE
(Tel: 01543-264303)

Spires View, 4 Friary Road, Lichfield, WS13 6QL (Tel: 01543-306424)

The Maples, 38 Balmoral Close, Lichfield, WS14 9SP
(Tel: 01543-255645)

8 The Close, Lichfield, WS13 7LD (Tel: 01543-418483)

The Hawthorns, 30 Norwich Close, Lichfield, WS13 7SJ
(Tel: 01543-250151)

LICHFIELD SERVICES

Post Office: Beacon Street

Banks with ATMs; Lloyds, HSBC, Barclays & NatWest, all in centre of town

Tourist Information Centre: Lichfield Garrick, Castle Dyke
(Tel: 01543-412112)

Transport connections: mainline railway station

LICHFIELD – PENKRIDGE

OS Map: Explorer 244

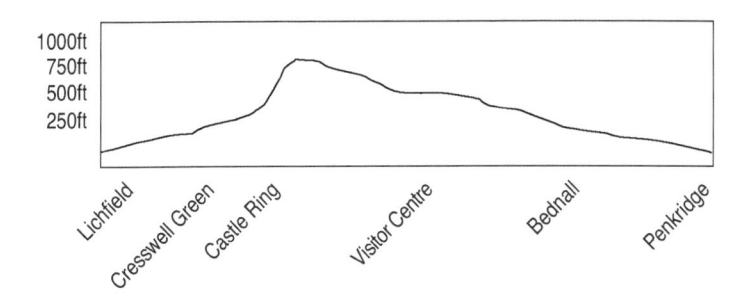

This is the longest section of the walk but it is not without considerable pleasures. For most of this day you will be following the line of the Heart of England Way, so waymarking is good. The route leaves Dr Johnson's Lichfield past the wonderful triple-spired cathedral and passes the one-time home of another of Lichfield's favourite sons, Erasmus Darwin, before leading across country to reach the ancient monument that is Castle Ring hillfort, the highest point on Cannock Chase

The highlight of the day is the stretch from Castle Ring across Cannock Chase, the United Kingdom's smallest Area of Outstanding Natural Beauty, where nature is allowed to flourish and whose Visitor Centre offers an opportunity for a mid-journey break. You leave the Chase via two War Cemeteries and a Memorial to call in at Bednall before this long day's walk ends with a stroll along the towpath of the Staffordshire & Worcestershire Canal into the ancient settlement of Penkridge.

PLACE	DAILY MILES	TOTAL MILES
Lichfield	-	13.5
Cresswell Green	3	16.5
Castle Ring	6	19.5
Chase Visitor Centre	9.5	23
Bednall	13.5	27
Penkridge	16.5	30

LICHFIELD to PENKRIDGE
(16.5 miles)

Lichfield – Cresswell Green (3 miles)

- Take The Close westwards from Lichfield Cathedral. At T-junction go right 150 yards on Beavon Street then left on Shaw Lane.
- Bend right through car park and walled alleyway then keep ahead through further car park and on path around edge of golf course to stile.
- Go ahead to further stile and carefully cross busy A51 on to path across field to Pipe Green gate. Follow right field boundary bending to cross footbridge and reach gate and path to road by Maple Hayes Hall.
- Go left, passing The Abnalls and Green End, till reaching stile in hedge on right. Go diagonally right across two fields with stile between to further stile.
- Follow left field boundary to stile then climb through three fields with stiles to reach Keepers Cottage at top of hill.
- Go right on road and continue on road forking right towards Chorley.
- Just after Brook Cottage but before entering Chorley, go left on path alongside brook through three fields with stiles between to cross plank bridge on to road.
- Go straight across on to road leading to Creswell Green.

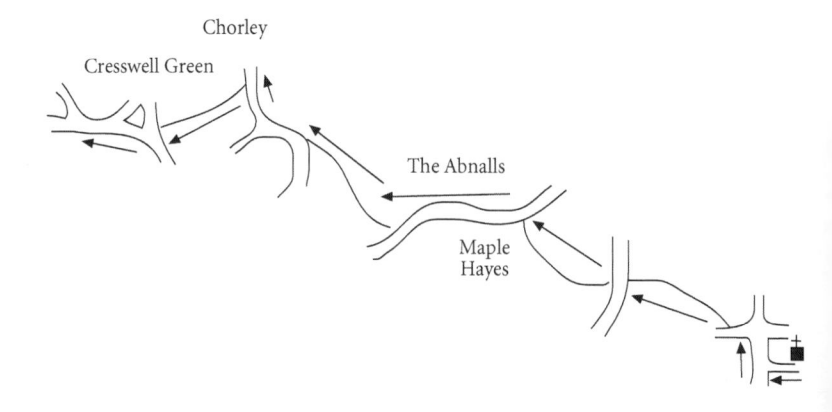

THE ABNALLS & MAPLE HAYES

The Abnalls was originally the home farm of Maple Hayes and was once owned by Erasmus Darwin, who created a botanic garden there. This was described by Anna Seward, author of Black Beauty, as 'a little, wild, umbrageous valley, a mile from Lichfield, amongst the only rocks which neighbour the city so nearly. It was irriguous from various springs, and swampy from their plenitude'. *When Darwin left Lichfield in 1781, the garden was looked after by a fellow-member of the Lichfield Botanical Society and later by Darwin's son Erasmus, the father of the famous Charles.*

Maple Hayes Hall is currently used as a school for dyslexic youngsters, which advertises itself as the home of the Morpheme and the Unisensory approach for the education of dyslexic children. At least they can spell those words!

CRESWELL GREEN

Although Creswell Green is a tiny settlement, it has been inhabited since 1380 when Henry of Cressewalle was assessed for tax, poor sap. Before that, even, John of Padbury owned land in Padbury Lane in 1298 and there are records of buildings here by 1775.

The Nelson Inn, however, is a more recent addition, dating back only to 1824. It is a popular local pub, despite being hidden away in the middle of nowhere, comfortably furnished and offering good drinks and food.

Creswell Green – Castle Ring (3 miles)

- At junction in Creswell Green go left then take right fork signposted Boney Hay just past The Nelson.
- After 100 yards go left on rising bridlepath, passing Bott's Pond on right, and follow to reach T-junction. Go straight across on to Springlestyche Lane.
- 100 yards past The Drill Inn take stile on right and follow right field boundary. Near end of field, take double stile on right and climb following right field boundary via three stiles to reach road.
- Go right to reach crossroads then immediately left on to second bridlepath on left through bracken, running parallel to road.
- Follow into Gentleshaw, passing Ye Olde Windmill on right, and emerge on to road by Christ Church.
- Continue ahead past primary school and take gate at top of Buds Road on to footpath through trees.
- Go ahead on drive towards house and, just before house, go left on footpath beside metal fence to reach road by entrance to Beaudesert Scout & Guide Camp.
- Go straight across on to Holly Hill Road and follow road to reach right turn into Castle Ring car park.

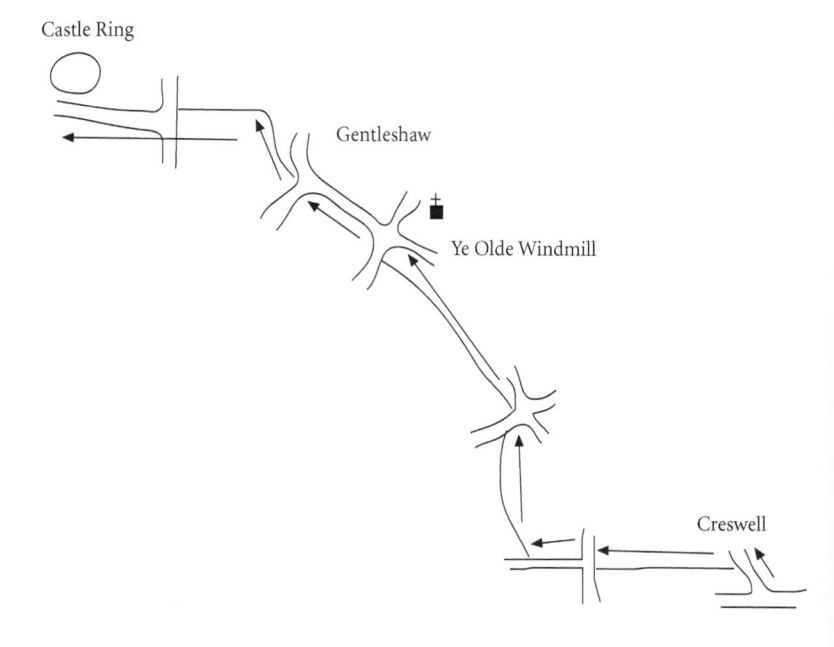

GENTLESHAW

Gentleshaw was originally the shaw or grove of John Gentyl who served the Bishop of Lichfield in the 14th century. There was once an abbey here, though the monks found the land (or the locals) too wild for them to tame and cleared off to Stoneleigh in Warwickshire. The abbey later became a royal hunting lodge, visited by bad King John, but there is now no trace of any building. The most memorable building in the area is what's left of the old windmill that is commemorated by a popular pub of the same name that sits close to it.

CASTLE RING

The village of Cannock Wood sits on top of the Cannock Chase coalfield that is the reason for its existence. The earliest records of coalmining on Cannock Chase are from the 13th century but it has been the major source of work for many centuries. At its peak in the early twentieth century the Cannock Chase coalfield was producing over five and a half million tons of coal annually. The first mention of the Cannock Wood collieries is in 1601, which is about the time when the village began to develop as well. It is now proud to be the only village wholly within the Cannock Chase Area of Outstanding Natural Beauty but do you care?

Castle Ring, just outside the village, is an Iron Age hillfort dating from about 500 BC. Its size suggests it was an important centre for settlers in the area. It is some 800 feet above sea level and its highest point gives extensive views of the surrounding countryside. It is said that, before the growth of trees on the Chase, you could see seven English counties and three Welsh ones (go on – try naming them).

Castle Ring – Cannock Chase Visitor Centre (3.5 miles)

- Go through car park and take signposted footpath to left of rampart. At crossroads of paths, go straight ahead and downhill to junction with broad track.
- Go right and continue descent, going straight over next crossroads of paths.
- At next fork by gas pipeline post, go left into valley bottom to join rising path. Continue straight ahead over next crossroads of paths to reach road.
- Go straight across road on to footpath opposite and follow past camping site on rising then falling path to junction with Marquis Drive *(named after the Marquis of Anglesey, who was second in command to the Duke of Wellington at Waterloo, where a cannonball took off his leg)*.
- Go left and continue on this broad track, ignoring all paths to left or right and passing sign for 'Moor's Gorse 1/2 mile', to eventually reach A460.
- Cross road and railway at Moor's Gorse *(one-time disembarkation point for RAF recruits going to RAF Hednesford)*.
- Continue ahead on ascending section of Marquis Drive known as Kitbag Hill.
- When track eventually levels out, go past site of RAF Hednesford with its commemorative stone and informative signage.
- Continue past entrance to Rangers' Office, then look for roadside sign for Cannock to left and follow to reach Cannock Chase Visitor Centre (01543- 876741).

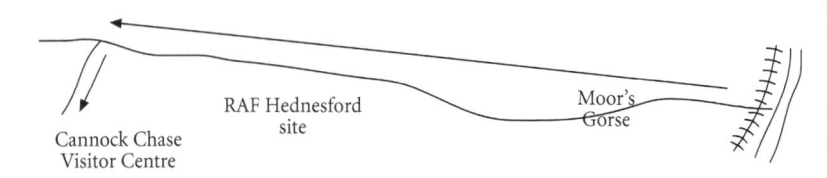

CANNOCK CHASE

Cannock Chase is what's left of a huge royal hunting forest, looked after for centuries by a royal-appointed Steward of Cannock Forest. It was designated an Area of Outstanding Natural Beauty in 1958, the smallest in Britain at 26 square miles. Much of the area is also designated as a Site of Special Scientific Interest. Within the bounds of the Chase you can find around 800 fallow deer, a variety of rare birds such as nightjars, yellowhammers and bramblings, and plants such as the eponymous Cannock Chase Berry.

There is a mass of paths throughout the AONB, suitable for and popular with walkers, horse-riders and cyclists. There are also several Visitors' Centres, notably the Cannock Chase Visitor Centre that offers a good mid-journey break, where you can sample excellent teas, coffees and homemade cakes (though sadly no ale). The White House Hotel further up the road is now a Baptist Retreat and offers only spiritual refreshment.

CANNOCK CHASE MILITARY HISTORY

Between 1914 and 1918 two huge Army Training Camps, connected by the Tackeroo railway, were built on the Chase and up to a quarter of a million British and Commonwealth troops received their basic training therein. The remains of these camps and the railways that supplied them are still evident in places. The Camps also contained a prisoner-of-war hospital to which many wounded soldiers were brought back from the Front.

In 1939 the Chase was commissioned once again for military use when RAF Hednesford was opened to provide basic training for thousands of men, living in huts such as the one next to the Visitor Centre. The camp remained open after the Second World War as a base for National Service training. Immediately after its closure it was recommissioned in 1956 to house Hungarian refugees fleeing from the Russian invasion of Budapest.

Cannock Chase Visitor Centre – Bednall (4 miles)

- Retrace steps to Marquis Drive and go left to reach T-junction with road. Go straight across road and follow footpath across common land to reach car park at Flints Field.
- Go right through car park and cross road to find further footpath opposite through trees. Go ahead, crossing crossroads of paths (*N.B. BT Tower to left*), then straight ahead to reach Penkridge Bank road.
- Go left for 400 yards then take footpath on right. At second crossroads of paths, go left and follow past German War Cemetery and Commonwealth War Cemetery to reach road.
- Go right on road for 400 yards then go right on bridleway.
- In car parking area after 30 yards go left on track and follow across other tracks till crossing ditch on to pebbled path.
- Go left to reach surfaced lane near Katyn Memorial (*50 yards on right and worth a visit*) and go left to crossroads.
- Cross road on to Spring Slade by Springslade Lodge Tearoom and continue down hill to reach A34.
- Go right along pavement of road then left on Common Lane into centre of Bednall.

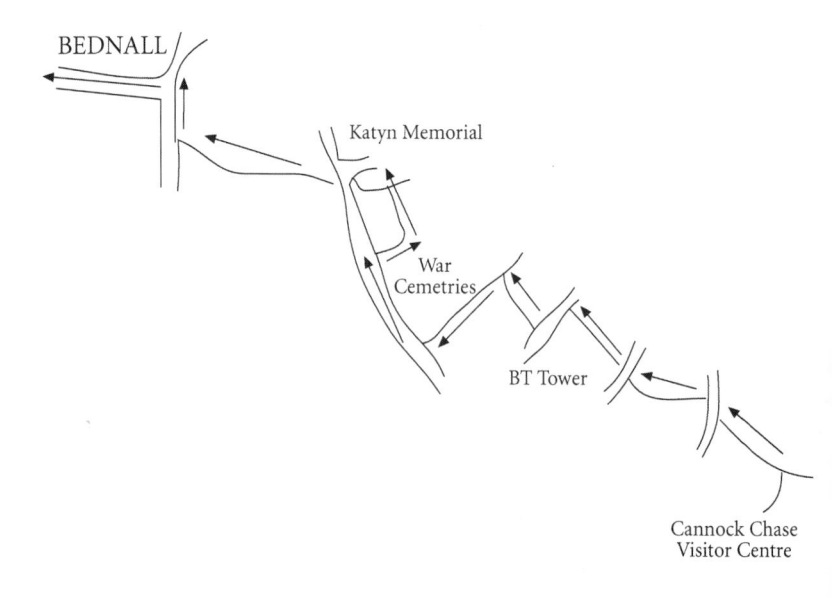

WAR MEMORIALS

There are three outstanding memorials to the folly of war on Cannock Chase. The German War Cemetery contains the graves of 5,000 German and Austrian soldiers and civilians who died in this country in both World Wars, plus a separate section for the crews of four airships shot down in the First World War. The cemetery was opened in 1967, when scattered graves across the country were brought into one place.

The Commonwealth Cemetery contains the graves of 97 Commonwealth soldiers, mostly from New Zealand, and of 286 German prisoners-of-war. The Commonwealth War Graves Commission maintains both of these cemeteries.

The Katyn Memorial was unveiled in 1979 by Stefan Staniszewski, whose father Hillary Zygmunt Staniszewski (a high court judge) died in the Katyn massacre at the hands of the Russian army. Preserved below the memorial are phials of soil from both Warsaw and the Katyn forest.

BEDNALL

The village of Bednall originates in the depths of history, being called Bedehala in the Domesday survey, but it remains a tiny settlement. Its present All Saints church, built on the site of a former chapel, was built in 1846 but incorporates some 12th century features.

Philip Alsop, a poet of the First World War, lived in the nearby vicarage where his father and grandfather had been the incumbents.

Bednall – Penkridge (3 miles)

- Go left by church on to School Lane becoming Cock Lane and continue past primary school and entrance to Moors Covert Farm on Staffordshire Way.
- At fork in roads by Gypsy Green Farm go right and after 100 yards go right again on signed footpath.
- After 75 yards at end of hedge, go diagonally left across field to stile into woodland.
- Take path over planks through trees to stile at edge of woodland.
- Go straight ahead across fields to reach stream and follow course of stream, eventually bending left, and then go right over footbridge.
- Go diagonally left across field to stile and go through boatyard to Park Gate Bridge. Cross bridge and double back right on to towpath.
- Continue on towpath, passing under M6 motorway, to reach Penkridge Bridge. Ascend to road by The Boat Inn and go right into centre of Penkridge.

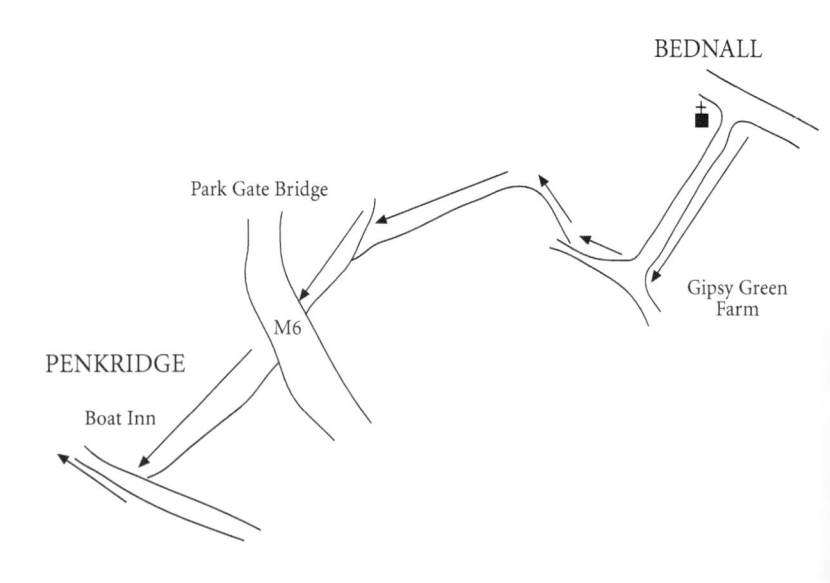

PENKRIDGE PIX

White Hart

Old Gaol

Penkridge Viaduct

Littleton Arms

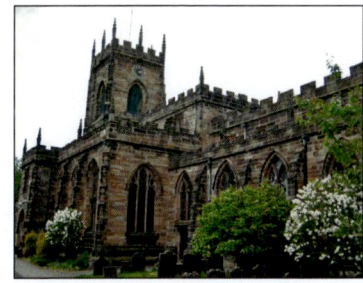

St Michael's

The Old Cottage

PENKRIDGE STORY

In a word I believe I may mark it the greatest horsefair in the world for horses of value.

Daniel Defoe

Modern-day Penkridge is dominated by the West Coast railway that speeds to the west of the village over a huge seven-arched viaduct, by the wide expanse of the A449 that once was the main connecting route from Birmingham to the Potteries, by the Staffordshire and Worcestershire Canal, and by the M6 that sweeps by in a deep cutting to the east. It owes its origins, however, to Roman times, probably for much the same reasons that these transportation routes cut through it nowadays, for it lies on flat ground that would have been obvious territory for marching through on the journey north and therefore provide grounds for the settlement of Pennocrucium.

Little is known about Penkridge's place in Mercian times, but it does appear that there was a large and powerful tribe known as the Pencersaetan based in Penkridge. The most interesting record of Penkridge past is in a charter of King Edgar, dated 958, which states that Edgar was in the village for one day and many claim that consequently for that day Penkridge was the capital of England. This may be a slightly exaggerated claim.

The red sandstone church of St Michael is the dominant building in the village, its origins lying over one thousand years ago in Mercian times. In medieval times it was one of a very few Collegiate churches in England and it contains monuments to the Wynnesburys, who were once Lords of Pillaton Manor, and the Littletons, who succeeded them. Inside the church is a Dutch wrought-iron screen, made from the gates of the Boer headquarters in South Africa and retrieved by one of the Littletons serving there.

In the 18th century the wealthy and powerful Littletons moved from Pillaton Hall to the newly-built Teddesley Hall where they received many notable guests, including the Duke of Wellington, Sir Robert Peel, Handel, John Wesley, Alexis de Tocqueville and Daniel Defoe. During the Second World War, Teddesley Hall was used to house American soldiers and later prisoners-of-war. Most of it is now demolished.

The current population of the village is 8500, the closeness of the rail and road networks allowing many of its citizens to work further afield in Birmingham and the Black Country or in Stafford. It still hosts a busy livestock market and a popular general market but unfortunately the greatest horse-fair in England described by Daniel Defoe is no longer.

PENKRIDGE CELEBRITIES

Edward John Littleton, Lord Hatherton (1791-1863)
The Littleton family of Teddesley Hall was the squirearchy of Penkridge, the Littleton Arms in the centre of the town being testimony to their importance in its history. Edward Littleton was MP for South Staffordshire at the time of the coming of the railways, benefiting financially from the creation of the Grand Junction Railway through his land and being able to require any train to stop at the station for him. Later, however, he fell out with the directors and his privileged access to trains at Penkridge station ceased almost immediately.

Thomas Brassey (1805-1870)
Thomas Brassey was actually born in Cheshire but his building of the Penkridge Viaduct for George Stephenson in the creation of the Grand Junction Railway has left a lasting landmark in the town and was the foundation stone of his later business and wealth. During his lifetime he was responsible for building one third of all the railways in the United Kingdom, over three thousand miles of railway in Europe and over fifteen hundred miles of railway elsewhere in the world. It is said that he accrued more man-made wealth than any other Englishman in the 19th century.

Elizabeth Gaskell (1810-1865)
Elizabeth Gaskell, the author of *Cranford*. was a regular visitor to Teddesley Hall and there came across the head gardener, a Mr Burton, whose extraordinary experience she wrote about in Charles Dickens's magazine *Household Words*. Burton had been appointed in 1848 to the position of head gardener to the Shah of Persia but, when he reached Tehran, he discovered that the Shah had died and his successor was not interested in gardening. A year of bad experiences followed, including attempted robbery and the witnessing of executions, before Burton returned to England and the safety of Teddesley Hall.

Eddie Straiton (1917-2004)
Eddie Straiton was the first of the TV vets. His broadcasting career began in 1957 when he was asked to give advice to farmers on animal health on *Farming Today* and subsequently he wrote a number of books as 'The TV Vet'. The high point of his broadcasting came when in 1977 he took up a regular slot on BBC Radio's *Jimmy Young Show*. A friend of James Herriott from their university days, Straiton advised the BBC on the filming of *All Creatures Great and Small*.

PENKRIDGE CAKES

DICKENS OF A TEA SHOPPE, *2 Crown Bridge*
Old-fashioned tea shop, as the name suggests, serving teas, coffees, homemade cakes and teacakes.

THE COFFEE SHOP, *Market Street*
Teas, coffees plus a selection of homemade cakes, scones and toasted snacks.

PENKRIDGE ALE

BOAT INN, *Cannock Road*
Lively, canalside pub popular with boaters. Open all day and has special curry nights, sizzler steak nights, quizzes etc. Wide choice of good pub grub served daily and range of Real Ales, including Speckled Hen, Abbot and Bombardier.

LITTLETON ARMS, *St Michael's Square*
The Inn rests on the cellars of the medieval Collegium guest house. Built with bricks of Penkridge clay and with Teddesley oak in the early 1790s by local craftsmen for Sir Edward Littleton, it became the centre of village life, hosting great balls, auctions, estate rent days and the magistrates' court.

RAILWAY INN, *Wolverhampton Street*
Opened for the business of the hundreds of Irish 'navvies,' who built the Grand Junction Railway in about 1835, because the navvies were banned from all the other pubs in the district. Past CAMRA pub of the month, serving Speckled Hen, Black Sheep, Banks's.

THE STAR, *St Michael's Square*
The Star traded as a public house until the 20th century when it became the Penkridge Co-op and then was a private residence but was restored to the licence trade in the second half of the 20th century. Serves food and range of Real Ales including Banks's, Jennings, Marston's plus Brakespear and Brains. Popular with locals.

WHITE HART, *Stone Cross*
Legend has it that both Queen Elizabeth I and Mary Queen of Scots visited the inn. Popular with locals and with visitors to Penkridge market. Serves food at lunchtimes only plus range of Real Ales including Banks's, Everard, Speckled Hen and Ruddles.

PENKRIDGE ACCOMMODATION

Bridge House Hotel, Stone Cross, Penkridge, ST19 5AS
(Tel: 01785-714426)

Hatherton House Country Hotel, Pinfold Lane, Penkridge, ST19 5QP
(Tel: 01785- 712459)

Littleton Arms, St Michael's Square, Penkridge, ST19 5AL
(Tel: 01785-716300)

Wolgarston Farm, Cannock Road, Penkridge, ST19 5RY
(Tel: 01785-715207)

PENKRIDGE SERVICES

Post Office: Market Street

Banks with ATM: Lloyds & Barclays, Stone Cross

Tourist Information Centre: None

Transport connections: mainline railway station

PENKRIDGE – ECCLESHALL

OS Maps: Explorer 244, 242 & 243

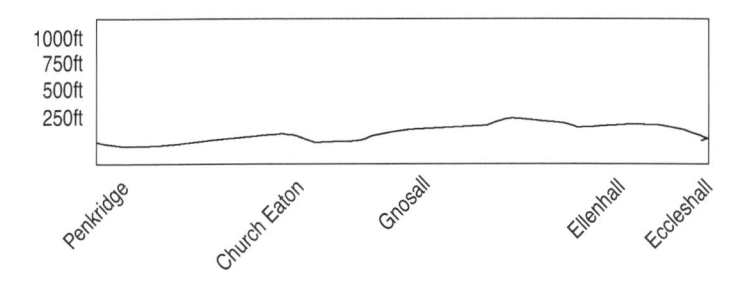

The third section of the trail takes you through lush agricultural country in Staffordshire's western side, going initially by lanes and fields to the Anglo-Saxon village of Church Eaton with its lovely old church of St Editha. A short trek across more fields brings you to the towpath of the Shropshire Union Canal for a steady walk into Gnosall, a large village split in two by the railway line that is now a footpath and cycle route. Here there is an opportunity for a mid-journey break at The Boat canalside pub and to top up on anything needed in the good array of village shops.

The latter part of the day continues heading northwards past the atmospheric ruins of Ranton Abbey and through the small settlement of Ellenhall, before following a long lane into the old coaching town of Ecceshall, once the home of the Bishops of Lichfield and an important stop on the London to Chester coaching route.

PLACE	DAILY MILES	TOTAL MILES
Penkridge	–	30
Church Eaton	6	36
Gnosall	9	39
Ellenhall	13.5	43.5
Eccleshall	15.5	45.5

PENKRIDGE to ECCLESHALL
(15 Miles)

Penkridge – Church Eaton (6 miles)

- From Littleton Arms take A449 northwards to cross bridge over River Penk. Immediately after bridge take road left to pass under last arch of railway viaduct. At fork in road go left on Preston Vale Lane.
- Continue on lane for a distance to reach cottages and postbox just before Preston Vale Farm. Go right over stile by Perton Cottage by sign saying 'Mitton 2 1/4 miles' and follow right field boundary round two sides of field to join farm track.
- Go straight ahead on wide track and continue till eventually bending right uphill to stile on left on to road. Go left on road into Mitton. At T-junction in Mitton go left again then immediately right on Shredicote Lane.
- Continue on road for a distance, bending right by Shredicote Farm. Opposite Shredicote Hall Farm go through gate and cross field to plank bridge and stile in hedge on to lane.
- Cross lane and go through gate on to bridlepath towards large oak tree and on same line to gate into Shredicote Wood. Follow clear path through woodland and at end of trees go straight ahead to follow right field boundary to reach road.
- Go left 50 yards then right on footpath round right edge of copse to post. Go right across field to stile near end of hedge. Follow left field boundary to double stile and plank bridge and continue across field to further double stile and plank bridge. Cross next field to stile and follow left field boundary to further stile.
- Go left over stile for 100 yards then right on broad track to emerge on road by Bellfields Farm. Go left and follow road into Church Eaton.

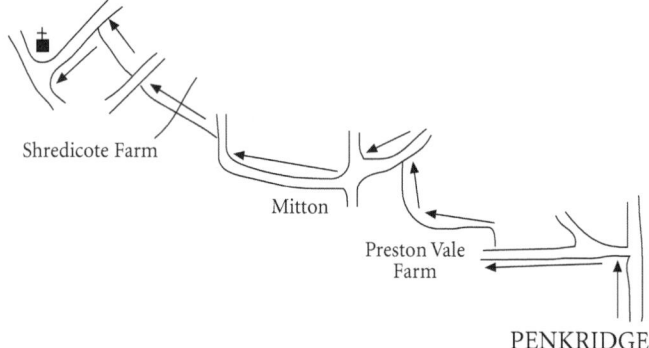

MITTON

Mitton was called Mutone in the Domesday Book and was one of ten places assessed as having 74 villagers with land for 17 ploughs. Make of that what you will.

Lower Mitton farmhouse is an early 18th century Grade II Listed building with 19th century additions. Made exclusively of red brick, it has a plain tile roof with a brick ridge chimney stack and an integral end chimney stack.

Some of its outbuildings have been turned into barn conversions but the farmhouse itself retains its 18th century attractions.

CHURCH EATON

Church Eaton was originally an Anglo-Saxon settlement and is recorded as Eitone in the Domesday Book. It is a big enough village to host its own website and its own Arts Festival, as well as offering many other activities to its community. Its pub, the Royal Oak, is unusual in being owned by a village consortium and is a real local with guest Real Ales, quiz nights and a popular restaurant.

St Editha's church dates from the 12th century although there was an Anglo-Saxon church on the site before then. The church is named after St Editha of Polesworth, the aunt of King Alfred and the daughter of King Egbert. The pilgrim route to Polesworth passed through Church Eaton; hence the name of the church.

Church Eaton – Gnosall (3 miles)

- At T-junction by St Editha's church opposite Village Institute go right to centre of village.
- At Royal Oak go right on road signposted 'Gnosall' and continue out of village to reach Brookhouse Farm.
- Just after farmhouse take footpath on left past barn. Immediately after barn go sharp right between trees to reach gate on to broad track.
- Go ahead on broad track to reach stile.
- Go diagonally right across field to metal gate at end of hedge line.
- Go ahead following right field boundary to join track rising to stile on to Bridge 28 of Shropshire Union Canal.
- Cross bridge and go right on towpath.
- Follow towpath under several bridges to reach Gnosall Wharf by Bridge 34 for Boat Inn (01785-822208) in Gnosall Heath.

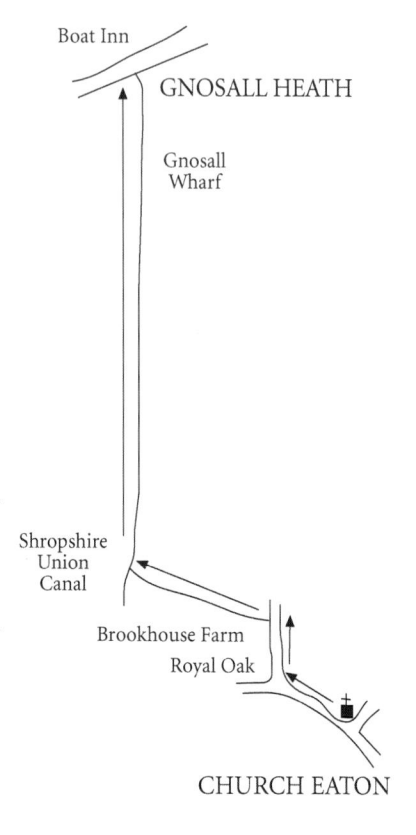

SHROPSHIRE UNION CANAL

The Shroppie, as it is known, came into existence in 1846 as an amalgamation of several canals running from the Midlands to the north-west, specifically from Autherley Junction to Ellesmere Port. The Shropshire Union Canal Society was formed in 1966 to preserve and improve the canals and, working with British Waterways, has been responsible for much valuable restoration and renovation.

The Boat Inn in Gnosall Heath is an excellent place for a mid-journey break, offering good food choices and a range of Real Ales, including Banks's and Jennings.

GNOSALL

Gnosall (pronounced Knowsall) is a large village split in two by the former Stafford to Wellington railway line, which is now a footpath. It has a population of 5,000 and all the amenities associated with such a population. Gnosall Heath lies to the south and abuts the Shropshire Union Canal while the old village of Gnosall is in the north, with many attractive buildings and local shops, including an excellent delicatessen/tea shop and the old village lock-up, kept as a warning to modern-day drunken youths.

The church of St Lawrence, dating back in parts to Saxon times but largely begun in the 13th century, is the dominant feature in the landscape.

Gnosall – Eccleshall (6.5 miles)

- Take Wharf Road to mini-roundabout in Gnosall. Go up High Street and continue through village ahead. Where Audmore Road goes right, go straight ahead on road to Brough Hall and Ranton. At first junction go left on Moorend Lane.
- Continue past Moor End up to farm. Go left past barn then continue to stile in left corner of field. Follow left field boundary to further stile.
- Go right, along right field boundary, rising then falling to stile in corner of field. Go diagonally right for 20 yards to further stile and plank bridge. Go through bushes to stile then cross field to two stiles in front of Hollyoak Farm to join broad track.
- Go left on track and after 100 yards go ahead through gate. Continue ahead across field to further gate, then follow right woodland boundary. At end of woodland keep ahead on footpath, with spectacular view of Ranton Abbey ahead.
- Continue on footpath through two gates on to track. Go right and just before Abbey go left through gate down to road, going through further gate.
- Cross road and go over stile to follow left field boundary to further stile. Continue following left field boundary to reach gate. Go ahead on broad track but, where track bends right, go ahead through further gate and climb through field to two gates.
- Continue ahead to cross farm track and reach gate by large post. Go diagonally left for 30 yards to gate then go right to gate on to road. Go right on road and at T-junction go left into Ellenhall.
- Continue on road for some way from Ellenhall to reach A5013. Cross road and go left on pavement to lead into Eccleshall.

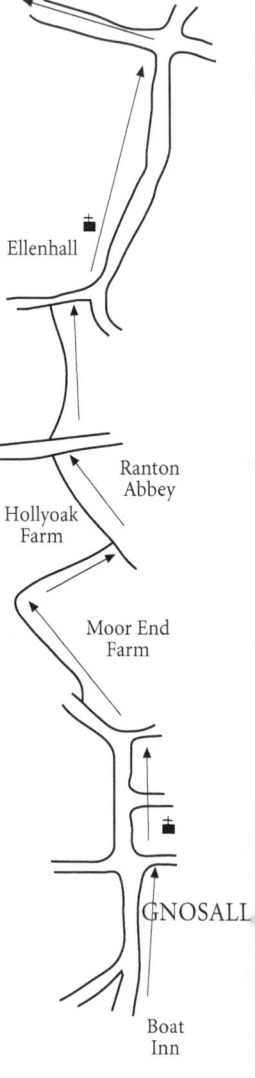

RANTON ABBEY

Ranton Abbey was founded around 1150 by Robert and Celestia Noel (such melodious names) as a subordinate house to Haughmond Abbey but all that is left of it today is the 14th century tower. There is a rumoured tunnel from beneath the Abbey tower to a farmhouse in Ranton.

Abbey House next to the Tower was built in 1820 as a hunting lodge and weekend retreat but it too is now a ruin, burned down accidentally during the Second World War by soldiers from the bodyguard of Queen Wilhelmina of the Netherlands who were stationed here (and presumably smoking pot!), close to the nearby headquarters of the Dutch resistance movement. It is a very spooky place, with the inevitable ghostly sightings attached to it, such as of a procession of medieval monks indulging in non-too-Christian practices. Be warned!

ELLENHALL

Ellenhall is a small sleepy village that was formerly part of the estates of the Earl of Lichfield. Ellenhall Grange Farm to the south of the village produces hand-made traditional bertelin cheeses (named after St Bertelin, patron saint of Stafford).

The church of St Mary stands on a small mound in the northerly end of the village. Its origins lie in the 12th century and the grey sandstone chancel dates from that time. The redbrick building you see nowadays owes itself mostly to the rebuilding completed in 1757 under the architect William Baker, a man much employed in Staffordshire.

The 17th century Ellenhall Hall beyond the church is brick-built and has a wealth of exposed interior beams; it is now a Grade 2 listed farmhouse.

ECCLESHALL PIX

Royal Oak

Holy Trinity

Bishop Overton's tomb

George Inn

Eccleshall Castle Tower

Slater's Queen Bee beer

ECCLESHALL STORY

(High Street) is an attractive street, even if it has no houses to make you stop.

Nikolaus Pevsner

At the heart of the town of Eccleshall is the 12th century Norman Holy Trinity church built on the site of several wooden predecessors, the oldest believed to have been founded by St Chad of Lichfield in the 6th century. The town's situation between the centres of the diocese in Chester, Coventry and Lichfield made it a natural home for the Bishops of Lichfield who lived here until 1867. Five bishops are buried in Holy Trinity church, namely Richard Sampson, Thomas Bentham, William Overton, James Bowestead and John Lonsdale.

The home of the Bishops of Lichfield was Eccleshall Castle, built originally after the Normans arrived and crenellated in the time of King John. It was used briefly in 1459 by Queen Margaret of Anjou as she was preparing to intercept the Yorkist troops heading for Ludlow. At the ensuing Battle of Blore Heath she was defeated with the death of many of the Lancastrian soldiers. In the Civil War Eccleshall Castle was besieged and partially dismantled by Parliamentarian troops. It was rebuilt in 1695 by Bishop Lloyd and is a substantial thirteen-bay brick house that still survives today, where it has been home for over one hundred years to the Carter family. The Castle is situated just north of the church, its nine-sided tower the main evidence of the old building.

Surrounded by rich agricultural land, Eccleshall became an important market town for produce and livestock serving this part of Staffordshire, although the market has now ceased. Its position on the main London to Chester route made it an important staging post in the days of coaching during the 18th century and most of the public houses in the centre of the town owe their origins to this period. Leather-working and shoemaking were the principal trades of the town, though both had died out by the end of the 19th century.

Farming is still a major occupation in this part of the world, but many local people commute to Stafford or Stoke for work purposes. The town has a good range of shops, restaurants and hostelries and several attractive Georgian houses and its High Street is a Conservation Area. Eccleshall is a regular winner of the Britain in Bloom competition and it holds a biennial show. Since 2007 the town has housed a biofuel power station using elephant grass, most of which is grown by local farmers.

ECCLESHALL CELEBRITIES

Richard Sampson (d. 1554)
Richard Sampson, whose tomb is inside Holy Trinity church, is the earliest of the five Bishops of Lichfield to be buried therein. He graduated from Cambridge in 1505-6, and became chaplain to Cardinal Wolsey and from then onwards he was deeply involved in affairs at the court of Henry VIII, being fortunate enough later to be supported by Thomas Cromwell, who obtained for him the position of Bishop of Coventry and Lichfield. Bishop Sampson's religious views were flexible enough for him to serve Henry VIII, Edward VI and Queen Mary – handy for him!

William Overton (1524/5-1609)
Bishop Overton was appointed Bishop of Coventry and Lichfield in 1580, having gained the favour of Robert Dudley, Earl of Leicester and Elizabeth I's alleged favourite squeeze. He arrived at Eccleshall Castle in debt and died in further debt. The only good thing he appears to have done is introduce glassmaking to the town when he invited the Huguenot glassmaker families of Tyzack and Henzey to move their trade thither. He had his own elaborate tomb constructed six years before his death 'in the hope of resurrection'. Some hope!

John Lonsdale (1788–1867)
In stark contrast to Bishop Overton, Bishop John Lonsdale was considered to be outstanding in terms of his moral rectitude. An exceptional scholar, who was appointed a Fellow of King's College, Cambridge, at the age of twenty-one, Lonsdale played a prominent part in the religious life of London for many years and was Principal of King's College, London. He became Bishop of Lichfield in 1843. Eccleshall's primary school is named after him.

Sarah Haggar (1851-1909)
Sarah Haggar was born in Eccleshall, the daughter of a proprietor of a travelling theatre. She is best known through her husband, William Haggar, whom she married in 1870 and with whom she had eleven children, each of them born in a different county of England and Wales. In the 1890s William became entranced with the new moving pictures, bought a camera and started making short films, often employing his wife and children as actors. The 1902 film, *The Maid of Cefn Ydfa*, was the family's first big success, followed by sixty others, including *The Life of Charles Peace* in which Sarah played the eponymous hero's mother.

ECCLESHALL CAKES

ARTISAN, High Street
Small but chic place, serving homemade pastries and cakes, and range of coffees and teas in a pleasant environment.

MACLEOD'S, High Street
Delicatessen with tables for teas, coffees, homemade cakes and other delicacies.

STAR CAFÉ, High Street
Teas, coffees, hot chocolate, cakes, sandwiches and hot snacks available.

ECCLESHALL ALE

BADGER INN, Green Lane
Double-fronted redbrick 19th century pub, serving Marston's, Holden's and Black Sheep. Dining pub with good range of food on offer.

BELL INN, High Street
Grade II listed former coaching inn, saved from conversion to flats by small beer company from Yorkshire. Pleasant beer garden for summer. Serves food from light bites to full meals and range of Real Ales, including Banks's, Titanic, Holden's, Everard, Timothy Taylor.

GEORGE HOTEL, Castle Street
Originally 17th century coaching inn but much renovated, though with flagstone floors and plenty of beams. Brewery tap of Slater's brewery (beers now brewed in Stafford), serving Original, Top Totty, Premium, Queen Bee etc. Serves highly-recommended food all day. CAMRA recommended.

KING'S ARMS HOTEL, Stafford Road
Another traditional old coaching inn with lots of separate rooms and real fires. Offers good food menu and range of Real Ales including Ruddles, Speckled Hen and Banks's.

ECCLESHALL ACCOMMODATION

Badger Inn, Green Lane, Eccleshall, ST21 6BA (Tel: 01785-850564)

Cobbler's Cottage, Kerry Lane, Eccleshall, ST21 6EJ
(Tel: 01785-850116)

George Hotel, Castle Street, Eccleshall, ST21 6DF (Tel: 01785-850300)

King's Arms, Stafford Street, Eccleshall, ST21 6BL (Tel: 01785-850294)

Peel House, 45 High Street, Eccleshall, ST21 6BW (Tel: 01785-859284)

ECCLESHALL SERVICES

Post Office, Stafford Street

Bank with ATM: NatWest, High Street

Tourist Information Centre: none

Transport connections: regular bus services to Stafford, where there is a mainline railway station

ECCLESHALL – STONE

OS Maps: Explorer 243 & 258

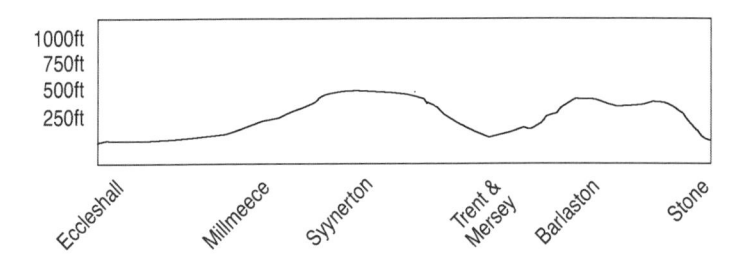

The trail is still heading northwards initially through rich agricultural land, passing what was once intended for use as a Regional Government Headquarters just outside Swynnerton. The village itself holds the key to a fascinating piece of royal history from the 18th century and its toposcope gives an outstanding viewpoint. Shortly afterwards, you begin to head eastwards to cross three major national transport arteries – the M6 motorway, the West Coast railway line and the Trent & Mersey Canal, where a good mid-journey break can be enjoyed at The Plume of Feathers.

The second part of the day takes you on a short loop along the Trent & Mersey Canal to the Wedgwood Visitor Centre just outside the village of Barlaston where you can marvel at the wonders that the great one-legged potter, Josiah Wedgwood, initiated in this part of the county. A pleasant climb over the National Trust-owned Downs Banks brings you finally into the bustling canal town of Stone.

PLACE	DAILY MILES	TOTAL MILES
Eccleshall	-	45.5
Millmeece	3	48.5
Swynnerton	5	50.5
Trent & Mersey Canal	9	54.5
Barlaston	11	56.5
Stone	14	59.5

ECCLESHALL to STONE
(14 Miles)

Eccleshall – Millmeece (3 miles)

- From crossroads in centre of Eccleshall take A519 northwards, keeping on left side of road and crossing River Sow. 200 yards after road turning to Swynnerton, take signed footpath left.
- After 100 yards go right through gate and then diagonally left down to gap in hedge. Go straight across next field to metal gate.
- Continue ahead over next field to further gate, leading on to broad concrete track. Follow past Spring Fields farmhouse to reach junction with Smithy Lane.
- Go right and, where lane bends left, go ahead over stile. Go straight ahead over two fields with stile between to reach road. Go left into hamlet of Brockton.
- Just past farm buildings go right and follow road to junction with A59 at Slindon with St Chad's church opposite.
- Cross road and go right 40 yards then left on Sytch Lane.
- Continue on this lane, ignoring all footpaths to left and right, to cross railway bridge over main West Coast line.
- At fork in roads, go right uphill through village of Millmeece.

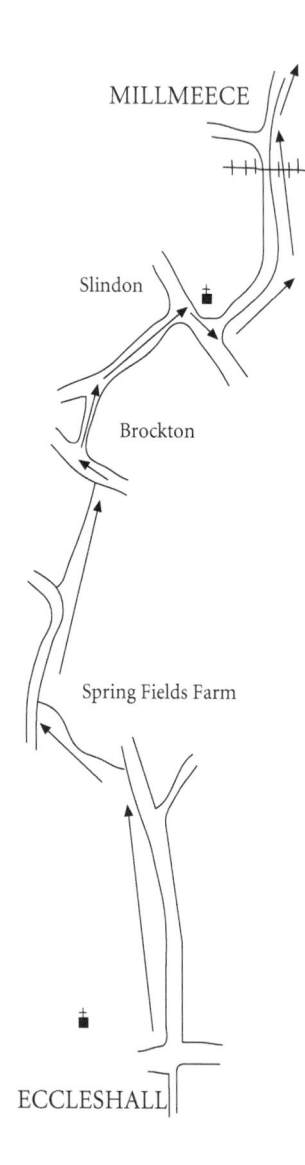

SLINDON

Slindon is little more than a hamlet with a few houses, a roadside fountain and the attractive church of St Chad. The latter was built in 1894 for J.C. Salt, a Stafford banker, by Basil Champneys, the well-known architect also responsible for Mansfield and Merton Colleges in Oxford, the John Rylands Library in Manchester and Newnham College in Cambridge among others. Pevsner calls St Chad's 'a little gem of a Late Victorian church' with its Gothic style and its stained glass windows by Charles Kempe. You can call it what you like.

MILLMEECE

Millmeece is a fairly non-descript village whose only claim to fame is its Pumping Station, situated just outside the village adjacent to the West Coast railway line. Water is raised at Millmeece by lift pumps that deliver water to an underground tank. From there the water is lifted further by ram pumps. Both the lift and ram pumps are powered by two horizontal tandem compound Corliss valve engines using steam raised by three Lancashire boilers. The efficiency of steam-raising is increased by a Green's economiser. It operated thus from 1928 to 1979 and is now operated by the Millmeece Pumping Station Preservation Trust.

Although you don't go past the Pumping Station, there will be a test on all this later.

Millmeece – Swynnerton (2 miles)

- Just past Holly Lodge where road in Millmeece ends, go left 30 yards then right over stile.
- Follow right field boundary to stile in top corner of field. Continue to follow right field boundary over further stile.
- Shortly after passing two small pools, take stile into copse and go left over further stile on to road.
- Go right on road past New Birch Farm, bending left by Gate 4 of Swynnerton Training Camp.
- At fork in roads at Cotes, go left and follow through settlement.
- Just past New House Farm, go right up steps to stile. Follow left field boundary over two stiles into copse.
- Go left in copse to gate then bear right across centre of field towards woodland
- Follow left edge of woodland to further gate. Continue ahead past cricket ground to stile on to road.
- Cross road and take alleyway between houses rising to road.
- Go left, following road past St Mary's Protestant church and Our Lady's Catholic church, to reach Fitzherbert Arms and shop in centre of Swynnerton.

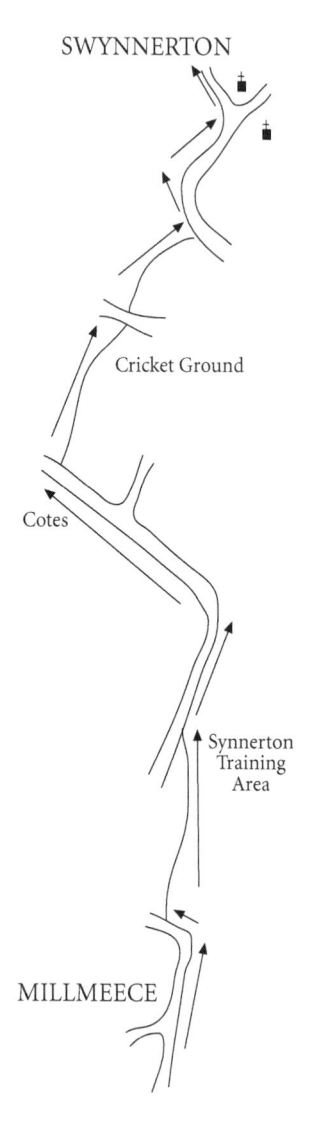

SWYNNERTON ROYAL ORDNANCE FACTORY

Now known as Swynnerton Training Area and used largely by army cadets and suchlike, Swynnerton ROF has an interesting history. It served from 1941 to 1957 as an ordnance factory, employing 5000 people in filling shells and other armaments, but was then mothballed, until from 1962 to 1964 it was reopened as the civil defence Group Control for North Staffordshire and Stoke Borough Council, later becoming the Staffordshire County Control and County Training Area.

In the 1980s much of the site was refurbished and in 1988 it became the Regional Government Headquarters for the eastern part of the West Midlands in case of nuclear warfare. Its bunker had accommodation for the regional commissioner and his immediate support staff, representatives from government departments and military liaison officers, who would be able to survive there for several months, till they died of boredom. It was closed in 1992 and sold back to the army.

SWYNNERTON

The Fitzherbert Arms in Swynnerton commemorates a remarkable woman, who lived in Swynnerton Hall, which stands on the site of a former great manor house that was destroyed in the Civil War. The Hall was the home for a short period of Maria Anne Smythe-Matthews who, on her marriage to the master of Swynnerton Hall, became Mrs Fitzherbert and, on his death, became the mistress and then in 1785 wife of the future George IV. Because she was a Catholic, the marriage was not recognised as legal in England, although the Pope declared it valid. George IV subsequently married Princess Caroline of Brunswick but his relationship with Mrs Fitzherbert continued unabated and she was his regular and lasting bedfellow. Swynnerton, which received its charter from Edward I in 1306, unusually has two churches – one Protestant and one Catholic, opposite each other.

Swynnerton – Trent & Mersey Canal (4 miles)

- Continue on road past Fitzherbert Arms. At first road junction, go left on road signposted Beech and Stableford. Continue on road, pausing to take in views of The Wrekin, Clee Hills, Long Mynd etc from commemorative stone toposcope *(557 feet above sea level)* opposite attractive water tower, which is now a house.
- On reaching A51, cross road and go right 30 yards then left on bridlepath, signposted Hanchurch Way. Continue on bridlepath to junction with Green Lane. Go ahead descending through woodland. At end of descent, go left on bridlepath between trees and follow to reach road. Go left into hamlet of Beech.
- At fork in roads, go right descending steeply into Beech Dale. At T-junction at bottom of hill, go sharp right and follow road past Beech Caves *(used for digging out sandstone, some of which was used to build Trentham Hall in 1633)* to cross M6 motorway.
- Continue on Beech Dale Road to junction with Winghouse Lane. Go left and follow through Tittensor village to Winghouse pub.
- Cross very busy A34 and go right. Immediately past black and white cottages, go left on Private Lane/footpath between houses to stile. Descend through field to reach bridge over River Trent. Continue straight ahead over three fields to three successive stiles on to road.
- Go straight across on to alleyway between houses. At road go right 20 yards then left on further alleyway to reach Plume of Feathers (01782-373753) by the Trent & Mersey Canal.

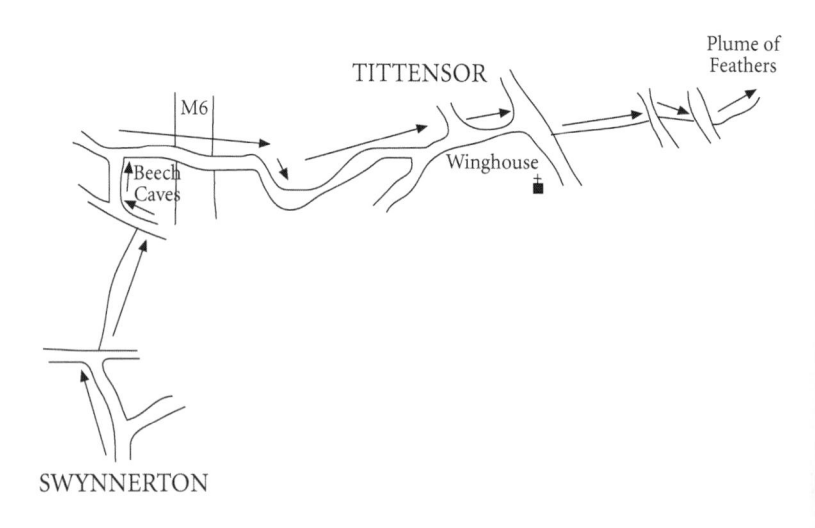

TITTENSOR

The foundation stone for St Luke's church in Tittensor was laid in 1880 by Millicent, Duchess of Sutherland and wife of the Marquis of Stafford. The architect, Roberts of Trentham, was mocked by one critic as being 'an amateur or an engineer or something' and the church was said to look like 'a Boulton & Paul ready-made'. The Tudor-style clock tower is certainly quaint. Inside there are some carved wood panels taken from the old manor house that was demolished in 1963.

The new Manor House is hidden behind a wall on the opposite side of the busy A34 but there are reputedly tunnels running under the road to the church.

TRENT & MERSEY CANAL

The Trent & Mersey Canal built to link the East Midlands, West Midlands and the North West was built by ace canal builder James Brindley, supported by Josiah Wedgwood who could see the enormous benefits of being able to transport his precious pottery-ware north, south and east. It stretches some 93.5 miles between Derwent Mouth in Derbyshire and the Bridgwater Canal at Preston Brook in Cheshire, whence it connects to the River Mersey. It was authorised by Parliament in 1766 and the first sod was cut by Josiah Wedgwood that same year. Eleven years later the Grand Trunk, as Brindley called it, was open with over 70 locks and five tunnels, including the 2926 yard Harecastle Tunnel near Kidsgrove in the city of Stoke-on-Trent. The towpath from Barlaston to Kidsgrove is now part of National Cycle Route 5.

Situated next to the canal is the Plume of Feathers, a popular and suitable mid-journey stopping place, which serves good food and a range of Real Ales, including Abbey, Green King IPA and Black Sheep.

Trent & Mersey Canal – Stone (5 miles)

- Go left on canal towpath outside Plume of Feathers. Follow towpath to Oldroad Bridge 104. Go up to road and go right.
- Cross railway at Wedgwood Station and continue past Wedgwood Visitor Centre *(bit pricey but worth visiting)*. Just past pool and estate road, take footpath on right over stile and head uphill towards tree. Continue across field to stile in top right corner.
- Go left past St John's church and the magnificent Barlaston Hall. Continue to junction of estate road with main road. Go ahead into Barlaston itself.
- At War Memorial go straight ahead on footpath towards Upper House Hotel. At bottom of hotel drive, go right through gate on to footpath and continue through further gate to climb up to woodland and gate into Downs Banks.
- Continue on path at top of woodland and eventually reach gate to begin descent. At bottom of descent, go right by stream to reach road and go right again on road.
- Just past Meaford Farm, take road left. At next fork in roads go right crossing stream. Where road bends left, go right on footpath into woodland and after 20 yards go right again on broad track.
- Follow track to steps up to gate, then go diagonally left across Common Plot to reach gate in bottom left corner of field. Cross road on to Whitebridge Lane.
- Cross railway and go ahead on road to reach canal bridge beyond Whitebridge Estates. Cross bridge and go right through hedge to reach towpath. Go right again and follow into Stone, heading for town centre from Bridge 94.

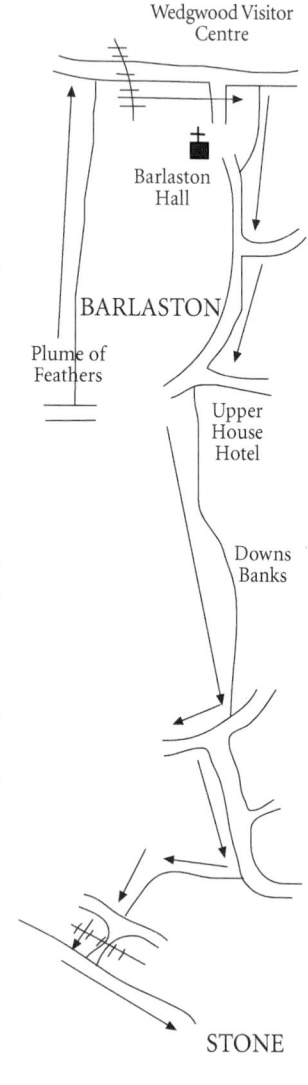

WEDGWOOD

Josiah Wedgwood, the father of English pottery, was a noted scientist, artist and engineer and member of the famous Lunar Society with such luminaries of the Industrial Revolution as Matthew Boulton, Erasmus Darwin and James Watt. Wedgwood founded his own pottery company in 1759 in Stoke, creating for his potters the model village of Etruria with its own housing and factory, in line with his social and political views. Thus began the Wedgwood Pottery Works that would dominate English ceramics for almost two hundred years.

The Etruria estate was wound down in the 1930s and a new village created at Barlaston, notable for the way the works are situated within rolling parkland. The Wedgwood Visitor Centre therein tells the fascinating story of Wedgwood pottery over the centuries.

BARLASTON

Barlaston is an old village, certainly dating back to Anglo-Saxon times as a pagan grave from 600 has been discovered cut into rock. It is first mentioned in the will of a certain Wulfric Spot, who was killed in battle against the Danes in 1012. The heron and coronet still used in the village sign stem from his coat of arms. Known as Benulvestone in the Domesday book, the village then had eight households and in five hundred years had only increased to eighteen households. Barlaston Hall was built in 1756 but the Wedgwoods planned to demolish it in the 1980s, only to be thwarted by a national campaign. The building has now been restored to its former glory.

The arrival of the Trent & Mersey Canal in the 1770s brought new industry, principally boat-building and chandlery, to Barlaston but the greatest expansion has occurred via new housing post-1945.

STONE PIX

Stone Railway Station

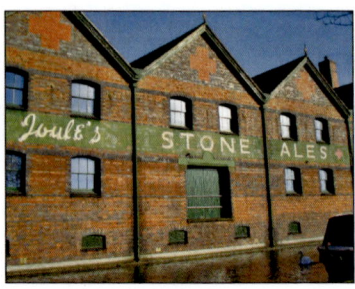

Former Joule's Brewery

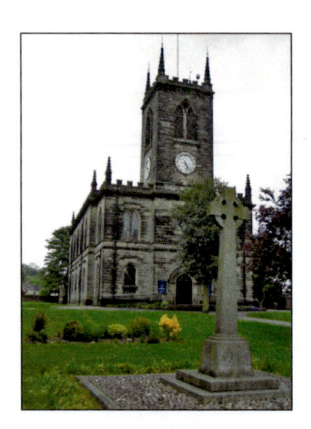

St Michael's

Swan Inn

Jervis Mausoleum

Sign on Trent & Mersey Canal

STONE STORY

Stone.. a very lively town, and a great thoroughfare for coaches, carriers and travellers.

1851 Directory

Although there was undoubtedly an Iron Age settlement here, Stone grew in importance in Mercian times, especially when Queen Ermenilda established a chapel here in the 7th century in memory of her two sons, Ruffin and Wulfad, who were murdered by King Wulfhere because they would not renounce their Christianity. Some say that the town takes its name from the stones that were raised from the River Trent to place on their grave. A later Augustinian priory on this site was established in AD 1135 but it collapsed in the 18th century and was replaced by the present church of St Michael's. A rib-vaulted undercroft from the priory still exists underneath Priory House near the church.

The town became an important staging post in the coaching days of the 17th century on the main route from London to the north-west. The Crown Hotel in the centre of the town was the recipient of up to forty coaches per day, providing a secure storage facility for post awaiting the next stage of its journey. The Crown also served as a gaol and from early in the 19th century as a customs and excise office.

It was in The Crown that Josiah Wedgwood met with Thomas Bentley and Erasmus Darwin in 1766 to commission James Brindley to build the Trent & Mersey Canal, necessary for transporting materials to Wedgwood's potteries in Stoke-on-Trent and for carrying finished goods north and south to market. The Trent & Mersey Canal offices were in Stone and the canal, with its two canalside pubs The Star and The Swan continues to be a major thoroughfare, although mostly for pleasure craft nowadays.

Because of the quality of its water beneath the town, Stone used to have two breweries – Joule's, whose office entrance can still be seen where the Co-operative Stores currently stand and whose phone number was Stone 1, and Bents. Fortunately, a microbrewery has now re-established the Joule's brand and its beers can be sampled in The Swan.

The coming of the railway made Stone into a backwater. Although it has a railway station, this was never a main stopping point and for many years it was closed. Since 2008, however, there are now regular services to north and south, although the main West Coast trains rush through without stopping. In some ways this has helped the town retain its identity as a small market town.

STONE CELEBRITIES

Admiral John Jervis, Earl St Vincent (1735-1823)
John Jervis was born just outside Stone. He entered the Royal Navy in 1749 and rose through the ranks to become captain during the American War of Independence, Admiral in 1795 and Commander-in-Chief of the British Mediterranean Fleet from 1796 to 1799 when he was made Baron Jervis and Earl of St Vincent. He was appointed First Lord of the Admiralty in 1801, where he made significant improvements to the administration of the Navy. In 1821 he was promoted to Admiral of the Fleet on the occasion of the coronation of King George IV. His mausoleum is behind St Michael's church.

Peter de Wint (1784-1849)
Peter de Wint was born in Stone, the son of an English doctor with Dutch forebears. In 1802 he was apprenticed to the portrait painter John Raphael Smith. He became friendly with the then-unknown John Constable and first exhibited at the Royal Academy in 1807. From then on he devoted his life to his art, becoming an acknowledged master in landscape painting, in oils and in watercolours. He has numerous paintings in Tate Britain, in the National Gallery and in the Victoria and Albert Museum.

Richard 'Stoney' Smith (1836-1900)
Richard 'Stoney' Smith invented a bread called Smith's Patent Germ Bread that was to revolutionise breadmaking. Smith, by perfecting a method of steam cooking, invented a genuinely new brown flour, rich in vitamins and nutrients. After a nation-wide competition, Smith's bread was renamed Hovis – taken from the Latin 'hominis vis' which means 'strength of man'. Its success was overwhelming – and by 1895, Hovis sales had reached 1 million loaves per week.

A.N. Wilson (1950-present)
Wilson is an English novelist, biographer and journalist, known as a Young Fogy, who was educated at Rugby and Oxford. His first novel was *The Sweets of Pimlico* (1977) and later works include *A Bottle in the Smoke* (1989) and *A Watch in the Dark* (1996). He has written biographies of Sir Walter Scott, Milton, Tolstoy and Betjeman. The last, published in 2006, included a hitherto unpublished letter detailing an unknown love affair, although this was later revealed to be a hoax as the letter included an acrostic that spelled out 'A. N. Wilson is a shit'.

STONE CAKES

CHATWIN'S COFFEE BAR, *High Street*
Serves a range of teas and coffees, plus homemade cakes and sandwiches. Small but personable local baker's shop.

HAMMERSLEYS OF STONE, *High Street*
Another local baker, serving a range of fairtrade coffees and herbal teas, plus homemade cakes and sandwiches. Has homely feel to it.

JACQUES CAFÉ & INTERIORS, *High Street*
Unusual setting for a café in midst of an interior design shop. Sit on the sofa then buy it! Serves a range of teas and coffees, plus cakes and sandwiches.

STONE ALE

CROWN & ANCHOR, *Station Rd*
18th century traditional thatched roof pub in centre of town, specialising in carvery with its Black Rock Grill for cooking your own steak. Serves range of Real Ales including Deuchars and Everard.

ROYAL EXCHANGE, *Radford Street*
Claims to be a Real Ale haven, with range of Titanic Ales plus regularly-changing guests including Everard. No music, just conversation.

STAR INN, *Stafford Street*
Voted pub of the Year by Mid-Staffs CAMRA, this canal-side pub is popular with locals and visitors equally. It has a number of differently-sized rooms with low ceilings, solid beams and stone floors. Serves range of Real Ales, including Banks's, Marston's and Jennings and food.

SWAN INN, *Stafford Street*
Grade II listed building converted from 1771 warehouse servicing Trent & Mersey Canal. Serves up to ten Real Ales including own Joule's ales (after local brewery). Also serves bar lunches, including free Sunday lunch buffet. Open all day. CAMRA recommended.

THREE CROWNS, *Lichfield Road*
Thatched former coaching inn on the edge of town, popular with passing boaters and cyclists. Good menu with food served till 10 pm. Range of Real Ales includes Banks's, Marston's, Jennings and Bass

STONE ACCOMMODATION

Couldrey's, 8 Airedale Road, Stone, ST15 8DW (Tel: 01785-812500)

Crown Hotel, 38 High Street, Stone, ST15 8AS (Tel: 01785-813535)

Field House, Stafford Road, Stone, ST15 0HE (Tel: 01785-605712)

Langtry's, 1-3 Oulton Road, Stone, ST15 8EB (Tel: 01785-813583)

Mayfield House B&B, 112 Newcastle Road, Stone, (Tel: 01785-811446)

Park Grange, Pingle Lane, Stone, ST15 8QT (Tel: 01785-816011)

Stone House Hotel, Stafford Road, Stone, ST15 0BQ
(Tel: 01785-815531)

Stowe House, Uttoxeter Road, Little Stoke, Stone, ST5 8QX
(Tel: 01785-813181)

STONE SERVICES

Post Office: High Street

Banks with ATMs: Lloyds, Barclays, HSBC in High Street, NatWest in Granville Square

Tourist Information Centre: None

Transport connections: mainline railway station

STONE – CHEADLE

OS Maps: Explorer 258 & 259

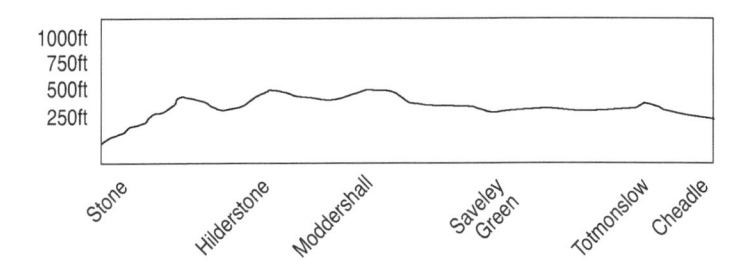

Stone is sometimes described as the gateway to the Staffordshire Moorlands and this section will give you a good introduction to these northern high lands. The trail begins with a cross-country switchback to the village of Hilderstone with its Elgar connections. Next it's across flatter country to Moddershall with its lovely duck pond in front of its pub, The Boar, and a gradual, tree-lined climb up through Idlerocks to Fulford and a well-earned mid-journey break at The Greyhound in Saverley Green.

A steady walk then brings you past the site of the great Catholic hideout of Paynsley Hall, sadly now no more than a memory, and up to the tiny but once-important settlement of Totmonslow. Finally there's a pleasant stroll across country and then climb through Huntley Wood to bring you in view of the market town of Cheadle and "Pugin's gem", the church of St Giles.

PLACE	DAILY MILES	TOTAL MILES
Stone	–	59.5
Hilderstone	3	62.5
Moddershall	5	64.5
Saverley Green	8	67.5
Cheadle	13.5	73

STONE to CHEADLE
(13.5 Miles)

Stone – Hilderstone (3 miles)

- Leave Stone via Church Street, passing St Michael's church and crossing the railway line. After the railway take second right turning into Redhill Road, quickly becoming a track.
- Continue on rising track, bearing left by entrance to Stonepark. At second stile continue straight ahead following left field boundary. After 300 yards go left over stile on descending path.
- Go over two stiles and footbridge over stream to further stile. Climb on wire-fenced path over several stiles to emerge on road opposite Home Farm.
- Go right on road, descending then climbing to find stile on left just past Wooliscroft Barns.
- Climb through field following left field boundary to stile by Wooliscroft Farm. Continue to follow left field boundary for 100 yards to reach stile in hedge on left.
- Go over stile and plank bridge and go diagonally right to gap in top right corner of field and continue through gateway beside Peakshill Farm.
- Go right and in middle of farm buildings go left. Aim diagonally right to top right corner of field for stile and continue on same line over next field to further stile on to road.
- Go left on Sytch Lane and at T-junction go left again into Hilderstone.

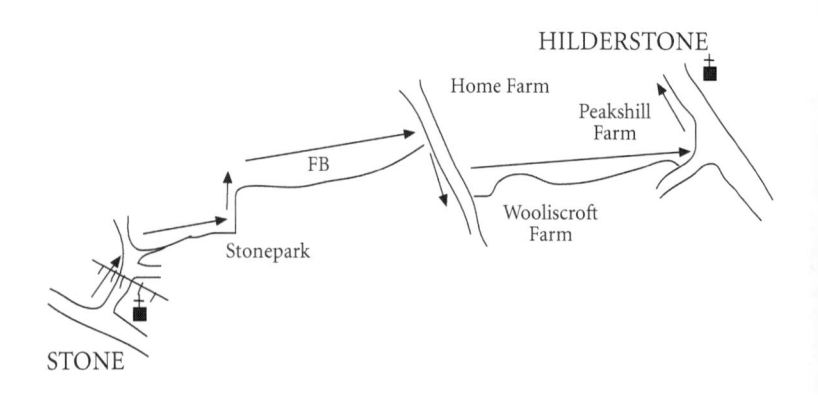

STONEPARK

Stonepark was the family seat of Earl Granville (1815-1891) who entered Parliament as a Whig in 1836, became under-secretary for foreign affairs in 1841 and Foreign Secretary in 1851. He was considered likely to become Prime Minister on two occasions but never made it to the top of the greasy pole, instead serving twice as Colonial Secretary (1868-70 and 1886) and twice as Foreign Secretary (1870-74 and 1880-85) to Gladstone. He was thought to be 'An urbane and well-liked man, but not an energetic politician'.

The family tomb is in the churchyard of St Michael's in Stone and he is further commemorated by Granvilles, a restaurant, music and comedy venue (which he would have loved!) in Granville Square in the town.

HILDERSTONE

Hilderstone, the place of the warrior wolf, dates back to the 7th century and signs of the Saxon strip and terrace farming are visible still in the village. The Domesday Book of 1086 attributes ownership of the village to Robert of Stafford.

Christ Church, built in the Gothic style and opened in 1833, has barely changed since then. It still has its forty-foot spire and only one bell, which is tolled every Sunday. Its glory is the East Window, made of enamelled glass and depicting Jesus consecrating the Mass. It is a rare example of work by the artist William Collins, father of well-known writer Wilkie Collins.

The son of the first vicar of Christ Church, William Meath Baker, was a friend of Edward Elgar, whose Fourth Movement of the "Enigma Variations" is dedicated to WMB (yes, him).

Hilderstone – Saverley Green (5 miles)

- Just past Roebuck Inn, go left on Dingle Lane, passing 1792 Bank Cottage and bearing right by Dingle Lane Farm. At end of lane, cross road and continue ahead on right field boundary, bending left to reach stile and footbridge on right.
- Go across field to find track by new plantation of trees. Follow track to end of plantation, then go over two stiles on to wire-fenced path to further double stile. Follow right field boundary to further stile.
- Go diagonally left and descend to stile. Follow left field boundary to further stile, then go straight ahead rising through field to stile on to road. Go straight across on to Marlpit Lane and at T-junction go right and follow road into Moddershall.
- Just past village hall and before reaching Boar Inn take second road on right, Rushtons Lane. At end of surfaced road go through gate and follow long woodland path through Idlerocks rising to stile.
- Over stile continue climbing to reach further stile in top right corner of field. Follow path over three stiles to reach road.
- Cross road and go over stile on to footpath through more woodland. At end of woodland go right on surfaced track and at T-junction go left towards Fulford.
- Take second left road, Baulk Lane. At first junction go left, then again left at next junction. Take next right past St Nicholas's church and through farmyard on to broad track. After 100 yards go over stile on left.
- Go diagonally right across field to stile in hedge, then diagonally left to plank bridge and stile in top corner of field. Go diagonally right to stile, then diagonally left to stile in bottom corner of field.
- After 20 yards go right over stile and follow footpath around caravan site to stile, leading to lane into Saverley Green near The Greyhound (01782-395576).

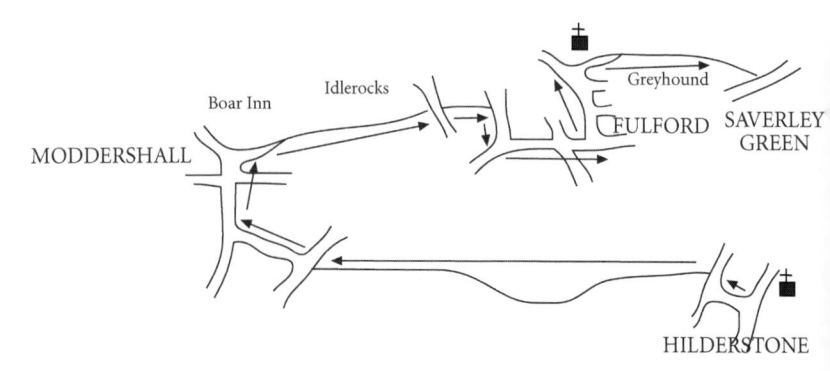

MODDERSHALL

Moddershall is a charming little village, centred upon All Saints church and the Boar Inn, which has its own duck pond. The village sits at the head of the Scotch Brook that travels three miles to Stone and on which there used to be nine mills, originally grinding corn but later retooled to grind flint for the Potteries. Splashy Mill is now incorporated into a private house and Mosty Lea Mill has been restored as a working mill by the County Council as an important part of our industrial heritage.

All Saints church was opened in 1904, paid for by three sisters of the Wedgwood family who lived nearby in Idlerocks. Curiously, the whole building was dismantled in 1993 because of subsidence and rebuilt using exactly the same stones, although with internal modifications.

FULFORD

Fulford is a village that has grown in size since the 1950s but its church of St Nicholas and neighbouring Fulford Hall stand on a rise above the new developments.

St Nicholas's was built in the 19th century on the site of a 15th century chapel. Its stained glass windows include one dedicated to St Chad, the first Bishop of Lichfield; he holds Lichfield Cathedral in his hand. St Nicholas's used to have a reputation as the Gretna Green of Staffordshire, because of the number of runaway marriages solemnised there. Ex-USA President Richard Nixon is descended from a Fulford family.

SAVERLEY GREEN

Saverley Green takes its name from the nearby Sale Brook. The tiny hamlet was once famous for cockfighting; in 1850 the police raided the site but the participants (and their cocks) fled into neighbouring houses and were not apprehended. The Greyhound is a very suitable place for a mid-journey break, serving a range of Real Ales, including Ruddles, Hobgoblin and Adnam's, and sandwiches.

Saverley Green – Cheadle (5.5 miles)

- Go left out of The Greyhound and follow road bending to junction with Sandon Road. Cross on to driveway and after 250 yards go left over stile to further stile.
- Follow stream for 50 yards then cross field to stile by large single tree on to surfaced track. Go right on track passing Leese House Farm and eventually entering grounds of Paynsley Hall Farm. Follow track bending left through farmyard. At end of farmyard bear left again to gate.
- Go through gate on to track to cross railway. Continue on surfaced track through Newton farms, passing under A50, to reach road opposite Totmonslow Farm.
- Cross road and go right. After 200 yards go left on Breach Lane into Totmonslow. Cross bridge over old railway and take track on left, bending right through farmyard to stile. Continue on broad track for 400 yards to reach marker pole.
- Go diagonally right to stile in bottom corner of field and stay on same line to next stile. Go diagonally left across field to stile in top corner then down to road. Go left under bridge and left at T-junction. After 50 yards go right up steps to stile.
- Climb to stile into Huntley Wood and continue on path. At first fork, go right descending and at second fork go left. Continue dipping and rising through wood to eventually reach marker post. Go right down to stile at end of Huntley Wood.
- Continue across field to stile on to road. Cross road on to footpath through woodland, emerging on driveway. Go left to cross road and take stile on left, then path to further stile. Turn left to stile and footbridge. Continue to metal barrier.
- After 20 yards go left into housing estate, crossing road on to surfaced path. Follow this path over further road, eventually bending right on to Glebe Road. On reaching junction with Town End, go right into centre of Cheadle.

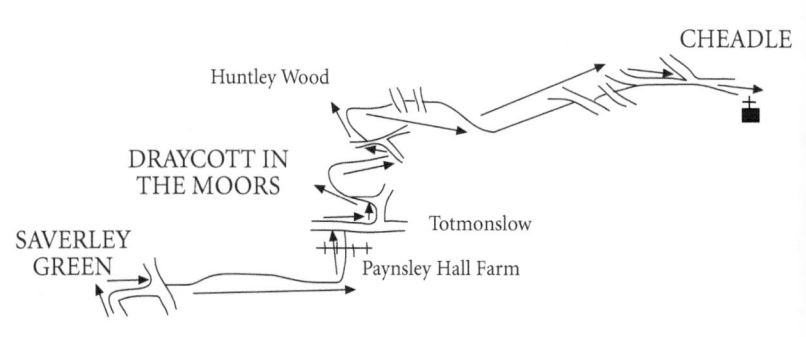

DRAYCOTT IN THE MOORS

Draycott in the Moors is a scattered village south west of Cheadle that incorporates the hamlets of Cresswell and Totmonslow. Its most infamous citizen has to be a shepherd named Joseph Reeves who allegedly lived to reach the age of 127 years. His secret, he claimed, was that 'he had never taken tobacco or physic, nor drank between meals, alleviating his thirst by rolling pebbles in his mouth'. *Poor sod!*

Cresswell is home to the Izaak Walton pub, named after the famous Stafford-born angler and author of The Compleat Angler, who is believed to have fished in the nearby River Blyth.

The unprepossessing settlement of Totmonslow was remarkably one of the five Hundreds of Staffordshire and marks the entrance to the Staffordshire Moorlands which in turn abut on to the Peak District. The area was abundant in natural resources, particularly lime, stone and coal. It once had a tumulus of a Saxon chief and the Roman road Richmild Street that runs through it is further evidence of its antiquity.

PAYNSLEY HALL

Paynsley Hall was the home of one of England's premier Catholic families, the Draycotts, after whom the nearby village is named. The family played important roles within Staffordshire over the centuries but, come the Reformation, Anthony Draycott the parish priest and his brother Philip refused to conform to the new Anglican religion. When Elizabeth came to the throne Antony Draycott was imprisoned in The Fleet, while his brother Philip maintained Catholic worship secretly in his chapel inside Paynsley Hall.

Philip's daughter Margery was married to Antony Babington, the ringleader of the so-called Babington Plot to assassinate Elizabeth and replace her with Mary Queen of Scots. Babington was subsequently arrested and executed. The original Paynsley Hall was pulled down on Cromwell's orders in 1644, leaving only the chimney and a wainscoted room. The last Draycott left England at the end of the 18th century but Catholic worship has continued in the area up to the present day, when Painsley Catholic College in nearby Cheadle is one of Staffordshire's leading schools.

CHEADLE PIX

Armillary Sphere

Market Buttery Cross

Tudor House Tearooms

Talbot Inn

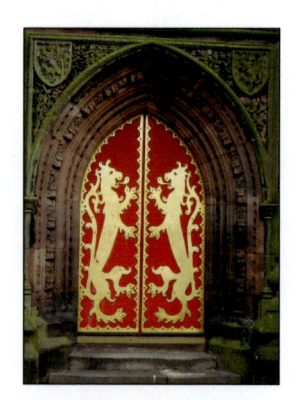

Lion Doors to St Giles

St Giles

CHEADLE STORY

Cheadle is Pugin-land.
Nikolaus Pevsner

Cheadle is a small market town in the Staffordshire Moorlands area, first mentioned in the Domesday Book as Celle, although it is probably of Anglo-Saxon origin. By the start of the 14th century there were seventy-five families using the corn-mill and by the late seventeenth century there were just over one thousand people in the town, growing to almost two thousand over the next one hundred years. Its population now is about twelve and a half thousand.

For most of its history Cheadle has served the needs of local agriculture and farming with its market, its 17th century market cross and the market place emphasising this point. Coal mining has also been an important trade in the area with over sixty mines operating at one time or another, although all are now closed. Other trades operating in Cheadle have been silk-making (William Morris of the Arts and Crafts Movement being a regular visitor to test out organic dyes), brass-making, tape-weaving and copper production; these too no longer exist.

The most prominent building in Cheadle is the Roman Catholic church of St Giles, designed by Pugin, who was given unlimited funds by the Earl of Shrewsbury, at the time Lord of the Manor at nearby Alton Towers, to build this church and the result was St Giles's, often referred to as 'Pugin's gem'. The church is the architect's own tribute to inner peace and serenity and a fine example of the Gothic Revival. On its opening day eight carriages carrying the Earl and Countess of Shrewsbury drove from Alton Towers to St Giles's to attend mass, together with eight deacons, fifty-three assorted Priests, thirteen bishops and two archbishops. I assume the Pope was otherwise engaged.

Modern-day Cheadle retains its market town feel, its High Street containing many attractive old buildings, some of whose survival looks at risk. The main sources of employment are agriculture still, the JCB factory and the nearby Alton Towers theme park, to which there is a regular bus service. The railway station is no more, finally closed to passengers in the 1960s and to freight in the 1980s, as the local sand and gravel companies changed to road transport. Interestingly the stone used to create the Thames Barrier was quarried around Cheadle and loaded on to trains at its station. The town's main asset nowadays appears to be in giving access to the surrounding hills, to the Churnet Valley and to the Staffordshire Moorlands.

CHEADLE CELEBRITIES

Augustus Welby Northmore Pugin (1812 –1852)
Pugin, the son of a French émigré architect, was educated in London but much influenced by his father's commitment to Gothic architecture. His early work was in designing furniture and carved metalwork but he moved on to produce important books about Gothic design. His conversion to Roman Catholicism brought him to the attention of Catholic patrons, who commissioned him to design buildings for them, which is how he came to create St Giles's church for the Earl of Shrewsbury. He is mostly remembered, however, for his rebuilding of the Palace of Westminster in London. Pugin died a young man, probably from the effects of syphilis.

Mary Adela Blagg (1858-1944)
Mary Blagg was an English astronomer and selenographer who became interested in astronomy in her middle age after attending a university extension course and commenced work for the International Association of Academies on lunar nomenclature in 1905, completing the work in 1915. She was the first woman to be admitted to the Royal Astronomical Society in 1916 and joined the Lunar Commission of the International Astronomical Union in 1920. The small crater Blagg on the moon is named after her.

Cecil Wedgwood (1863-1916)
Wedgwood was the great-great-grandson of Josiah Wedgwood and became a partner in the family business. He was commissioned Lieutenant in the North Staffordshire regiment in 1883 and served in the Boer War, receiving the Distinguished Service Order in 1902. He was mayor of Stoke-on-Trent in 1910 and 1911 and raised the 8th Battalion of the North Staffordshire Regiment at the outbreak of the First World War. He was killed at La Boiselle during the Battle of the Somme in 1916 and buried at Bapaume Post Military Cemetery.

Les Oakes (1938-2000)
Les Oakes started attending auctions with his grandfather when he was seven years old, buying and selling horse-drawn vehicles. By the time he was eleven, he had acquired, unknown to his father, over 70 horse-drawn vehicles, which he stored at various farms around Cheadle. In 1965 he moved to Hales View Farm and continued building his collection. By the time of his death he owned over 600 horse-drawn vehicles, including gypsy caravans, stationary engines and vintage vehicles, kept in his private Hales View Farm museum.

CHEADLE CAKES

MOSHI COFFEE BAR & GALLERY, High Street
Trendy and popular coffee shop with an art gallery, offering the high quality blend of the East African Moshi coffee bean, plus cakes etc.

TUDOR HOUSE TEAROOMS, High Street
Traditional tea room, housed in a Tudor-fronted building dating back to 1558. Offers a great selection of classic British cream teas and much more.

VICTORIAN TEAROOMS, Moorland Walk
Pleasant café that serves sandwiches and baguettes plus homemade cakes, speciality teas and coffees.

CHEADLE ALE

MASTER POTTER, Tean Road
Large open plan lounge as well as a separate bar area with pool and darts. Serves pub food from extensive menu and range of Real Ales including Abbot, Hardy & Hanson's Olde Trip.

QUEENS ARMS, Queen Street
Originally opened for local textile workers and became headquarters for pigeon-fanciers for many years. Serves range of Real Ales. CAMRA recommended.

SWAN, Townend
Once popular with miners, pub was refurbished in 1998 and serves a range of Real Ales including London Pride, Abbot Ale, M&B Mild and Titanic. Games room for darts, crib, table skittles. Also serves food.

THE HUNTSMAN, The Green
Recently re-opened pub popular with locals. Serves food and range of Titanic Ales and changing guests. Free wi-fi, plus monthly folk music sessions. CAMRA recommended.

CHEADLE ACCOMMODATION

Park Lodge Guest House, 1 Tean Road, Cheadle, ST10
(Tel: 01538-753562)

Park View Guest House, 15 Mill Road, Cheadle, ST10 1NG
(Tel: 01538-755412)

Railway Inn, 111 Froghall Road, Cheadle, ST10 2DN
(Tel: 01538-754782)

Royal Oak, 69 High Street, Cheadle, ST10 1AN (Tel: 01538-753116)

The Manor, 1 Watt Place, Cheadle, ST10 1NZ (Tel: 01538-753450)

CHEADLE SERVICES

Post Office: Cheadle Shopping Centre

Banks with ATM: Barclays, HSBC and NatWest in High Street

Tourist Information Centre: Councils Connect, High Street
(01538-483860)

Transport connections: regular bus services to Stoke-on-Trent where there is a mainline railway station

CHEADLE – UTTOXETER

OS Map: Explorer 259

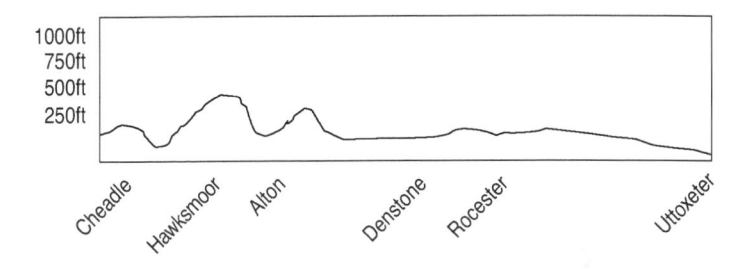

The first part of this section of the trail provides some of the most challenging walking as it leads over hill and dale from Cheadle to join up with the Staffordshire Way by East Wall Farm and then climbs through Hawksmoor Wood, through Stoneydale and Dimmings Dale to reach the village of Alton, with its infamous offshoot Alton Towers. Then there is a straightforward and level stroll largely along the route of the disused Churnet Valley railway line to bring you into the attractive village of Denstone where The Tavern provides a good opportunity for a mid-journey break.

The trail rejoins the Staffordshire Way in Denstone for a pleasant cross-country path following the River Churnet into Rocester, once a Roman fort but now the headquarters of the massive JCB empire, prominent on your approach. Then there's a steady walk though fields and meadows to reach the village of Stramshall before a final trek into the horse-racing town of Uttoxeter.

PLACE	DAILY MILES	TOTAL MILES
Cheadle	-	73
Hawksmoor	2.5	75.5
Alton	5.5	78.5
Denstone	8	81
Rocester	10	83
Uttoxeter	14	87

CHEADLE to UTTOXETER
(14 Miles)

Cheadle – Hawksmoor (2.5 miles)

- Leave Cheadle via Queen Street (B5417) and follow past Queen's Head. Take first left, Churchill Road. 50 yards after King Edward Street go right on footpath and follow into housing estate.
- Go left on Ness Grove, right on Lomond Grove then left on Tay Close. Take footbridge on right over stream and follow path behind houses to stile. Continue following right field boundary *(N.B. Hales Hall and Hales Hall Pool on right through trees)* over two stiles on to Cherry Lane.
- Go left on lane past entrance to Woodhead Hall Farm. Immediately after passing Woodhead Angling Club pool go right.
- Follow lane bending through The Woodhouse gated development and down to reach road.
- Cross road and go over stile. Descend to further stile and keep descending to cross stream. Bend left and continue on clear level path to further stile.
- Immediately after stile follow footpath sign left and downhill to further stile. Follow path around hillside to reach pool by East Wall Farm.
- Go right uphill following signpost for Staffordshire Way to join farm track around East Wall Farm over cattle grids.
- Enter Hawksmoor Wood and at fork in paths, go right and follow track climbing steadily through woodland to reach B5417 road opposite Greendale Lane.

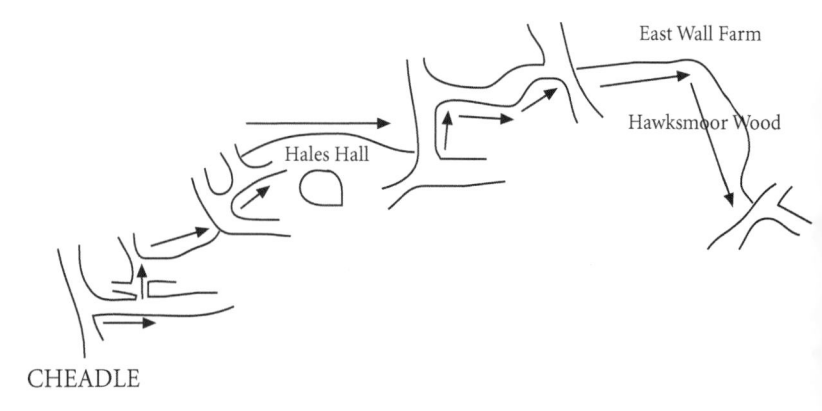

CHEADLE

HALES HALL

The redbrick Hales Hall was built in 1712 for the granddaughter of Chief Justice Matthew Hale, an influential judge at the time of the English Civil War. According to Pevsner, it has an exceptionally swagger front (as did Marilyn Monroe).

Nearby Hales Hall Pool is a man-made body of water that was created in 1846, probably to supply mills further downstream. It is now a fine example of a wetland ecology and has a broad path around it allowing visitors to observe the wildlife (waterfowl, dragonflies and damselflies) and plants (tussock sedge and lower reedmace). The view of the pool from the east looks back at Cheadle with the 200-foot spire of St Giles's church very prominent.

Hales Hall Caravan Site now occupies the garden of Hales Hall. Opposite it is the private museum that houses the Les Oakes collection of vintage carriages.

HAWKSMOOR NATURE RESERVE

Hawksmoor Nature Reserve, now managed by the National Trust, was founded by John Richard Masefield, who had been president of the North Staffordshire Field Club four times in its forty-nine year history. According to the memorial plaque on the gates into the Reserve, he was 'a great naturalist with an unrivalled knowledge of the flora and fauna of his native country'. It was opened in 1933 by his cousin, the Poet Laureate John Masefield. I must go down to the trees again!

Hawksmoor – Alton (3 miles)

- Go left on road for 100 yards then cross road and take footpath signed to Stoneydale.
- Continue on rising track and at summit of hill go left at fork in paths, descending to reach road.
- Go right on road. On reaching top of rise, go left on surfaced lane, climbing initially then levelling out.
- Keep ahead on lane, ignoring other tracks, until reaching large YHA sign. Immediately after sign, go left on descending path through woodland.
- Path becomes broad track and levels out beside attractive Woodland Lake, leading into Dimmings Dale beside Ramblers Retreat.
- Go past Ramblers Retreat and take rising path to right of road. On joining bridlepath, go left and follow, gradually descending to rejoin road by Holme Farm.
- Go straight across road and take stepped path into Toothill Wood. Climb to summit and go over stile.
- Turn right between walls for 30 yards then go left on broad track *(N.B. splendid views of Gothic Alton Castle)*. Follow track to emerge by Royal Oak in Alton.

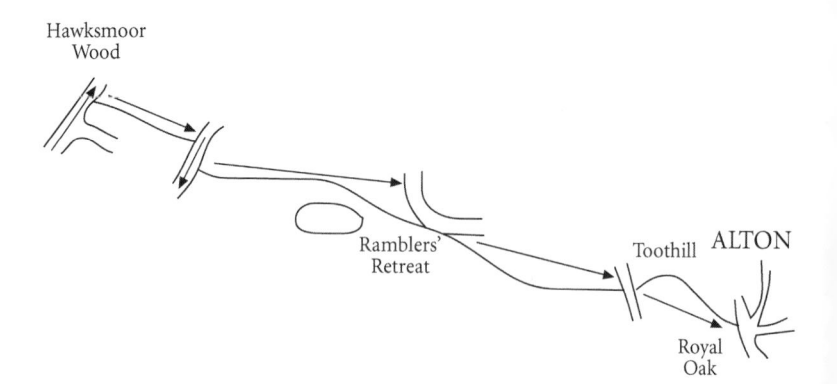

ALTON

The village of Alton with its fairytale castle sits high on the hillside above the Churnet valley. Originally a Saxon settlement, the village achieved its status when Bertram de Verdun built his castle here in 1175. What is visible now is the remodelled castle created by Pugin for the Earl of Shrewsbury n 1847, together with the adjoining church of St John (originally a hospital). The castle is now a Catholic Youth Retreat Centre.

St Peter's church was also originally built by Bertram de Verdun, although it was extensively remodelled in Victorian times. A number of remarkable wall paintings were uncovered during 20th century restoration work. One of these is believed to represent The Three Living and The Three Dead from an allegorical legend that originated in France in medieval times and warning that all, rich and poor, are equal in death. Even those who go to Alton Towers.

ALTON TOWERS

Alton Towers began life as Alton Lodge and was part of the Earl of Shrewsbury's estate before being bought by a group of local businessmen in the 1930s, who turned it into a park with gardens. After the Second World War, when it was used as an army camp, the building lay empty for many years until 1970 when it was opened as a theme park. It now attracts two and a half million suckers every year to queue up for such excitements as Nemesis (inverted roller-coaster), Oblivion (vertical drop roller-coaster), Air (flying roller-coaster), Rita (launched roller-coaster that reaches 100 mph in 2.2 seconds) and Th13teen (vertical free fall drop roller-coaster). Can you believe your luck to be passing by?

Alton – Denstone (2.5 miles)

- Cross road by Royal Oak and take second left Malthouse Road.
- Where road bends right, go ahead on descending footpath to reach road.
- Go left and follow pavement downhill on winding road. Opposite Alton Bridge Country Inn and before crossing River Churnet, go right on footpath into woodland.
- Just before Cliff Farm, go diagonally left over stile on path descending to footbridge. Go left over bridge and over field to stile leading to old Churnet Valley railway line.
- Go right on easy route of old railway line for some distance, passing footbridge over Crumpwood Weir on left.
- After going under stone road bridge over track, continue ahead to reach end of line in former Denstone station.
- Go right into Denstone village for The Tavern (01889-590847) and Post Office.

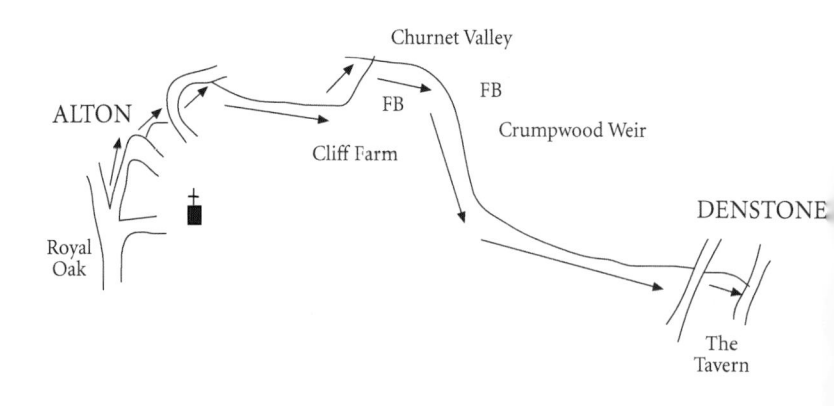

CHURNET VALLEY

The Churnet valley was a hotbed of industrial activity between the 16th and 19th centuries, filled with furnaces, mines and mills. The first mill was opened in 1573 at Oakamoor, the first furnace in 1593 at Dimmings Dale. It was a source of iron ore, copper, lead, coal, sandstone and limestone, while the River Churnet supplied water power and the surrounding woods provided charcoal. Currently the only industrial use of the Churnet is by the sand quarry at Oakamoor and the water quality has improved so much that salmon are being re-introduced to the river.

Part of the route takes you along the disused Churnet Valley railway line through scenic splendour, for this part of the county used to be known as Staffordshire's Rhineland. Low stone walls on either side of the track lead you eventually to where Denstone station used to be.

DENSTONE

The attractive village of Denstone is surrounded by the Weaver Hills, their highest point being some 1200 feet above sea level. It is a regular winner of the Staffordshire Best Kept Village award, indicative of its active and caring community. Its great benefactor was Sir Thomas Heywood, a Manchester banker who settled here in 1840 and paid for the present church and the old village school. He was also involved in the founding of the independent school, Denstone College, just outside the village.

All Saints church is of a Gothic design, built by the famous architect G. E. Street, who also created the Royal Courts of Justice in London and many other churches throughout England. Street was responsible for employing as his apprentice William Morris, who later became one of the founders of the Arts and Crafts movement.

Denstone has a Post Office, a farm shop with a café and a pub, The Tavern, which has a very good reputation and is a suitable place for a mid-journey break (N.B. no food on Mondays).

Denstone – Rocester (2 miles)

- From The Tavern go left and left again on to College Road, then left again past Denstone Hall and All Saints church to junction with B5032.
- Go right and immediately after crossing Quixhill Bridge go right again on footpath signposted Rocester.
- Cross two long fields with stile between to stile and footbridge. Continue ahead to stile by gate.
- Go diagonally left rising to stile into woodland and follow path rising through woods over two footbridges to emerge over stile into field.
- Go right and gradually descend to stile by gate and go up to traffic island. Take second road left towards Rocester.
- After 200 yards go right through gate and follow path past JCB monument *(known as The Fossaur, it is made with JCB digger buckets and arms)*. Emerge at footpath on Churnet Bridge and go right under main road.
- Go left on surfaced path around Mr Bamford's lovely duck pond. Continue on path, bearing right past JCB works to join road.

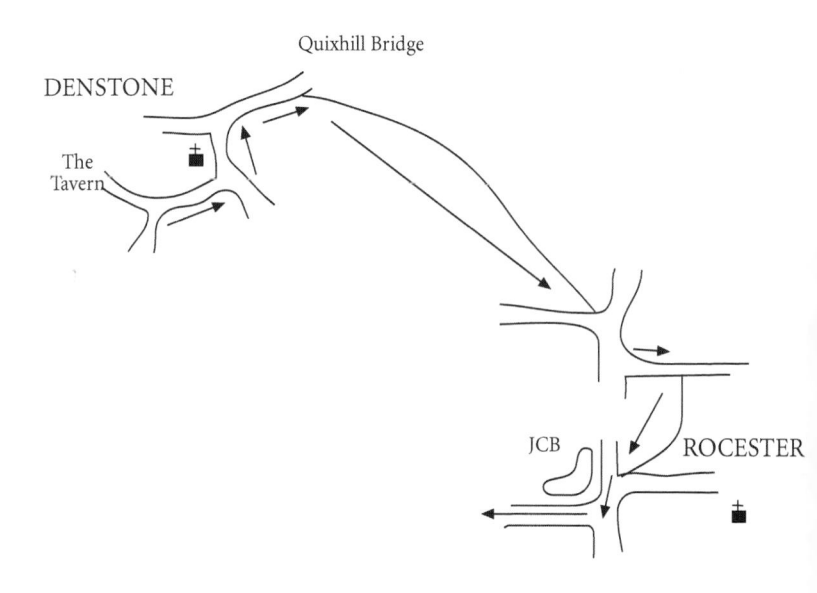

ROMAN ROCESTER

Rocester was originally, as its name suggests, a Roman settlement, a fort being built here in AD 69, most likely as a defence against the Brigantians. The Brigantians had originally been a trusted client of Rome and their Queen Cartimunda was an important ally who handed Caractacus over to the Romans. However, after she divorced her husband Venutius and replaced him with a muscle-bound armour-bearer, Venutius drove her out of the kingdom. The Roman army came to Cartimanda's aid and created the Rocester fort.

Excavations in the 1960s revealed the line of a military turf rampart near the current church. Various finds of Roman articles have been made in Rocester, including pottery, coins, a paved stone surface and a rare beautiful enamel brooch depicting a man on horseback. These can now be viewed in the Potteries Museum and Art Gallery in Hanley.

JCB IN ROCESTER

After the Augustinian Abbey was knocked down in the Dissolution in the 1530s, Richard Arkwright's purchase of an old corn mill on the eastern edge of the village next to the River Dove and its transformation into a water-powered cotton mill was the first major development in Rocester (pronounced Roaster) and the mill was still providing employment until the 1980s.

It is impossible to enter the village nowadays, however, without coming across the huge development of JCB World Headquarters in their superbly landscaped grounds.

The JCB works, which came here in the 1950s, has continued to expand ever since and now employs some 7,000 people worldwide, offers over 300 machines and claims to be one of the world's top three manufacturers of construction equipment. Why would you argue with that?

Rocester – Uttoxeter (4 miles)

- Continue on road for approximately half a mile, passing road to Stubwood, and take surfaced track opposite Four Winds cottage. At end of driveway go ahead over stile to further stile into woodland.
- Go ahead and take left fork to end of trees then sharp right through three gates. Descend to stile in bottom right corner of field.
- Go left and shortly after Combridge Farm go right over stile. Go ahead over three fields with stiles and climb to further stile by Lowfields Farm. Continue on same line over five fields with stiles between to reach stile on to Hook Lane.
- Go straight ahead on road. Where road bends left at Creighton Farm, go ahead through three gates and over two fields to reach stile at top of field and surfaced footpath between houses into Stramshall.
- Go left on Hollington Lane and left again on St Michael's Road by St Michael's church. Go right by Hall Farm through village centre on road becoming track past Stramshall Farm.
- Where track ends, descend to end of hedge on left. Go left to stile and continue on path over two more stiles. Twenty yards after second stile go right over stile and diagonally left to stile into Paragon Travel yard in Spath.
- Go right up to traffic island on A50. Carefully cross road and follow Town Centre signs into Uttoxeter.

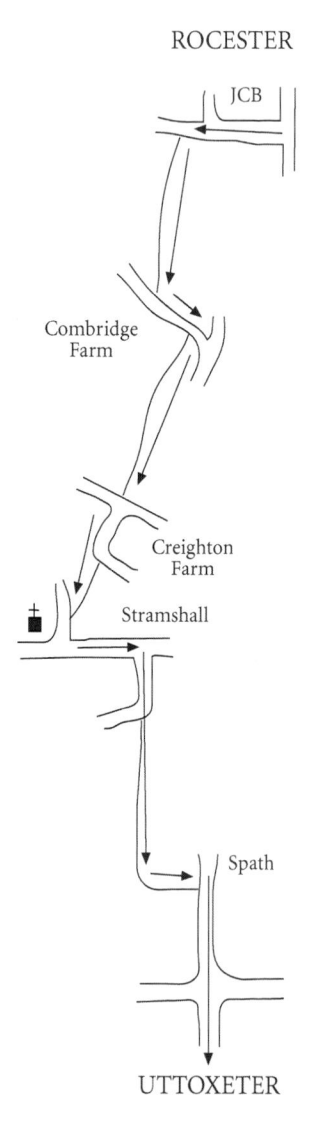

STRAMSHALL

Stramshall can be dated back as a village to the 13th century but there have been Romano-British pottery finds in the area. There was once a Quaker burial site, known as 'Quaker's Bit' in the village near the church of St Michael and All Angels, which was built in 1850.

Nearby Crakemarsh Hall, now only evidenced in its Lodge Gate House, was the home of the Cavendish family. Tyrell Cavendish, his wife Julia and her maid were on the Titanic when it sank. Tyrrell Cavendish drowned but his wife and maid were rescued from a lifeboat. Mrs Cavendish worshipped in the church for many years afterwards. The Hall, which was occupied by US troops during the Second World War and later by Italian POWs, was demolished in 1998 after a fire.

UTTOXETER CANAL

The short-lived Uttoxeter Canal used to run through Spath on the outskirts of Stramshall and there are traces of it still visible. The canal was an extension of the Caldon Canal and ran from Froghall in the north to Uttoxeter in the south. It was commissioned in 1797 but did not open until 1811 and it closed in 1849, in order that the Churnet Valley Railway could be built along its line. The United Kingdom's first automatic, train-operated level crossing was in Spath on that railway line. Wowee!

The railway has, of course, now long gone and in recent years a feasibility study into re-opening the Uttoxeter Canal has been developed, although its route would have to be modified as the old canal ran right through what is now the JCB headquarters.

UTTOXETER PIX

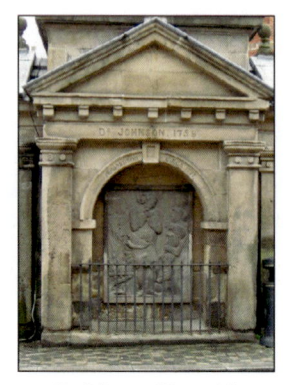

Dr Johnson Memorial

Heritage Centre

Uttoxeter Centaur

Uttoxeter Racecourse

St Mary's RC

Market Square Millennium Monument

UTTOXETER STORY

Uttoxeter was born on high ground above the flood plain of the River Dove.

Uttoxeter Online

Although Bronze Age axes have been discovered nearby and there is evidence of a Roman settlement in the area, Uttoxeter is an Anglo-Saxon settlement, its unusual name meaning Wittuc's homestead in the heather, and it has been spelled at least seventy-nine different ways over time. By the 15th century Uttoxeter and the lands of the lower Dove valley were renowned for their dairy products, some of which were sold at Uttoxeter market in butter pots made in the Potteries. Major fires of 1596 and 1672 destroyed most of the town's timber-framed houses, although on both occasions the town was substantially rebuilt. In 1648 the last surrender of the Civil War took place in the town when the Duke of Hamilton submitted to General John Lambert. Hamilton was executed three months later.

The market place is still the dominant feature of Uttoxeter, surrounded as it is by hostelries and containing the domed Weighing House where once goods would be measured and weighed for sale. On one side of this is a memorial to Dr Johnson whose father ran a bookstall in the market on which the young Samuel refused to help. In his sixties, Johnson returned to do penance by standing on this spot in the rain without a hat. Uttoxeter Market celebrated seven hundred years of existence in 2008. The nearby Maltings shopping precinct stands on the ground where once Bunting's brewery operated.

The town has a mainline railway station, dating back to 1881, and good bus connections. Just outside the town to the south-east and bordering the railway line is Uttoxeter Racecourse, which has been holding race meetings since the late 18th century and hosts twenty-five race meetings every year. Its most well-known race is the Midlands Grand National; Rag Trade, a 1976 winner, and Lord Ghyllene, a 1997 second placer, have gone on to win the Grand National at Aintree.

Uttoxeter residents are known as Uxonians and its most famous son, Joseph Bamford, set in train the development that is now the major employer in the area, JCB with its distinctive yellow logo. Fox's biscuits (previously Elke's and Adams) are the other large employer, Elke's being notorious for inventing the Malted Milk biscuit (yes!). An alternative view of the town is given in the film *This is England*, directed by Uxonian Shane Meadows, which follows a young boy growing up on a rough estate during the 1980s.

UTTOXETER CELEBRITIES

Henry Yevele (1320-1400)
Uttoxeter-born Henry Yevele was the greatest English mason of the late medieval period, leaving behind a treasure chest of buildings. His first royal commission is thought to be Kennington Manor in 1357 for the Black Prince and he was commissioned to work on the Bloody Tower at the Tower of London and on the clock tower of the Palace of Westminster. He worked in Westminster Abbey and Canterbury Cathedral, as well as the castles at Carisbrooke, Winchester, Portchester and Southampton. From 1368 he served as one of the two wardens of London Bridge.

Mary Howitt (1799-1888)
Mary Howitt was an English poet who wrote the poem *The Spider and the Fly*. She was educated in the family home in Uttoxeter and started writing at an early age. When she was twenty-two she married William Howitt and the two then embarked on a life of literary authorship. *The Lobster Quadrille* in Lewis Carroll's *Alice's Adventures in Wonderland* is a parody of *The Spider and the Fly*. You may prefer it.

Joseph Cyril Bamford (1916-2001)
Joseph Bamford began JCB in 1945 in a garage in Uttoxeter, using a welding set and some air-raid shelter materials to make his first tip-up truck. He moved the business to Rocester in 1950 and started painting his vehicles yellow. JCB's hydraulic tipping trailers became the market leader, conquering the USA from 1960 onwards and other parts of the world later. Bamford retired in 1975, making his son the managing director. The business is now worth some two and a half million pounds.

Bartley Gorman (1944-2002)
Between 1972 and 1992 Bartley Gorman was Bareknuckle Champion of Britain and Ireland and known as the King of the Gypsies. Originally from Bedworth near Coventry from a family of bareknuckle fighters, Gorman became involved in fighting early on, initially in the school playground and then in the gym of Bedworth Labour Club. He was a big man, standing over six feet tall and weighing over fifteen stone and became known as a ferocious fighter. He won his title in 1972 and maintained it for twenty years against numerous opponents in secretly-arranged fights where huge bets were placed. He retired in 1992 and settled to a more comfortable life on the outskirts of Uttoxeter.

UTTOXETER CAKES

INDULGENCE, *Lion Buildings, Market Place*
Wide range of exciting, homemade cakes (many gluten-free) plus coffees and speciality teas. Special treat is hot chocolate but also serves Staffordshire Oatcakes with various fillings. Yummy place to go.

LEAF AND BEAN, *Carter Street*
Near Heritage Centre, offers an amazing range of teas and coffees, while coffee is freshly ground on the premises. Also offers a selection of homemade cakes etc.

SADDLERS, *Old Saddlers Yard*
Offers traditional food, teas, coffees and sandwiches.

UTTOXETER ALE

BANK HOUSE HOTEL, *Church Street*
Once the town's first bank but now tastefully converted into hotel, using bank vaults as restaurant. Bar serves range of Real Ales including Abbot, Timothy Taylor and Pedigree. CAMRA recommended.

OLD STAR, *Queen Street*
Known for its friendly atmosphere and family orientation during week though can be busy at weekends because of live music on offer. Good juke box. Serves range of Real Ales, including Tribute, Spitfire and Hobgoblin.

OLD SWAN, *Market Street*
Wetherspoons pub but sympathetically refurbished, including watercolours by local artist. Offers usual range of Real Ales including Bass and Lymestone, plus range of well-priced food.

THE OLDE TALBOT, *Market Square*
Very old pub clearly full of history and with lots of cosy nooks but also full of flatscreen TVs on every wall. Serves range of Real Ales.

THE VAULTS, *Market Place*
Attractive frontage with etched windows leading to single bar inside. Old-fashioned pub that serves range of Real Ales, including Bass.

UTTOXETER ACCOMMODATION

Bank House Hotel, Church Street, Uttoxeter, ST14 8AG
(Tel: 01889-566922)

High View Cottage, Toothill Road, Uttoxeter, ST14 8JU
(Tel: 01889-568183)

Hillcrest Guest House, 3 Leighton Road, Uttoxeter, ST14 8 BL
(Tel: 01889-564627)

Oldroyd Guest House, 18-22 Bridge Street, Uttoxeter, ST14 8AP
(Tel: 01889-562763)

Ro-an-Mor B&B, 8 Stafford Road, Uttoxeter, ST14 8DN
(Tel: 01889-568566)

White Hart Hotel, 6-8 Carter Street, Uttoxeter, ST14 8EU
(Tel: 01889-562437)

Woodgate House, Wood Lane, Uttoxeter, ST14 8JR
(Tel: 01889-566488)

UTTOXETER SERVICES

Post Office: Carter Street

Banks with ATMs: Lloyds, Barclays, HSBC, NatWest in town centre

Tourist Information Centre: Heritage Centre, Carter Street

Transport connections: mainline railway station

UTTOXETER – BURTON-UPON-TRENT

OS Maps: Explorer 259 & 245

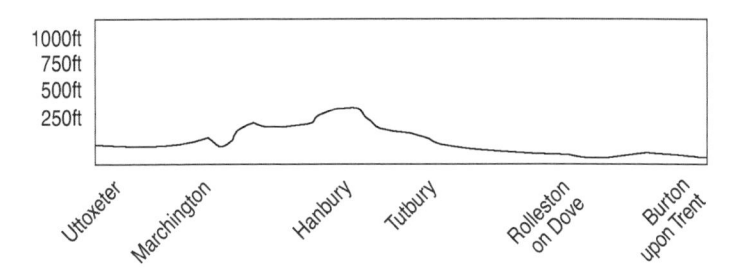

The final section begins gently with a stroll through meadows beside the River Dove before climbing up to the village of Marchington and then continues to climb through Draycott in the Clay to finally reach the fine church of St Werburgh in Hanbury. A well-walked path brings you to the site of the 1944 Fauld Explosion, when an underground bomb storage depot killed large numbers. The trail then takes you to the ancient town of Tutbury whose castle, where Mary Queen of Scots was imprisoned, invites you from a long way out and where The Old Dog & Partridge offers a final mid-journey break.

An easy journey across country from Tutbury to the attractive village of Rolleston-on-Dove brings you on to the Jinny Nature Trail and then along the towpath of the Trent & Mersey Canal into Burton-upon-Trent, the centre of brewing and the end of the trail.

PLACE	DAILY MILES	TOTAL MILES
Uttoxeter	-	87
Marchington	3	90
Hanbury	6	93
Tutbury	9	96
Burton-upon-Trent	14	101

UTTOXETER to BURTON-UPON-TRENT
(14 Miles)

Uttoxeter – Marchington (3 miles)

- From Centaur Island go down Brookside Road beside railway station to gate at end of road. Follow track bearing right behind racecourse. At fork in paths, go left and after 20 yards go right alongside stream over plank bridge to stile.
- Continue ahead broadly parallel with railway line through fields over stile and two plank bridges. After second bridge go slightly left up to further plank bridge and follow telegraph poles to stile and on to gate.
- After gate bear diagonally right to cross stile past bend in River Dove. Continue ahead over plank bridge and past Langridge rail crossing. Continue close to railway across fields over plank bridge and through two gates, passing two more bends in River Dove.
- Midway through next field take stile on right and carefully cross railway line over two stiles. Go left to footbridge and then take rising path to stile. Go right to reach stile beside stables on to road.
- Go straight across on to broad track. Where track ends go ahead across middle of field to stile and plank bridge. Go left descending to further stile and plank bridge.
- Go left again and follow path descending beside stream to road. Go left on Bag Lane and follow as road bends right past Bull's Head into Marchington.

UTTOXETER

MARCHINGTON

RIVER DOVE

For most of its forty miles the River Dove forms the boundary between Staffordshire and Derbyshire. Its journey begins on Axe Edge near Buxton and it travels generally in a southerly direction to join the River Trent at Newton Solney. On its way it flows through a number of limestone gorges, the best known of which is Dovedale which stretches from Hartington in Derbyshire to Ilam in Staffordshire and which is a major tourist attraction.

The Dove is famous as a trout stream and it was fishing in it that inspired Izaak Walton to write The Compleat Angler, *first published in 1653.*

MARCHINGTON

The village of Marchington has a long history dating back to Saxon times. It had a priest named Ellis in the 12th century and the present St Peter's church, built in 1744, has a medieval beam and chest from that period. In 1941 an American army base was built in the village with the vicarage becoming the headquarters and officers' mess. After the Americans left in 1944 for the D-day invasion, the army base became a prisoner-of-war camp.

Marchington is famous for a crumbling short cake once made here, which gave rise to the description of someone with a crusty temper being 'as short as Marchington wake-cake'.

It was also famous for its treatment of wife-beaters, with husbands being set astride a pole and carried on the shoulders of villagers to be judged by an elected committee. If found guilty, they were paraded through the village on the pole preceded by the town crier reciting their misdeeds. Happy days.

Marchington – Hanbury (3 miles)

- At T-junction after passing Bull's Head go straight across through gate on to footpath. Keeping to left, cross cricket ground to stile and footbridge. Go right to stile then left across playing fields to gate on to road.
- Go left 100 yards then right over stile and follow rising path to stile. Go right through hedge then follow left field boundary rising to stile. Go through trees then follow path to right of trig point, descending to trees. Follow left field boundary.
- Join broad track coming in from farm on left and follow to gate on to road. Go right past Dovegate Prison and Moreton to eventually reach Ashes Lane.
- Go right on road and right again at next T-junction. Opposite Highfield Farm, go left over stile and then diagonally right rising to stile in top corner of field. Go over stile opposite and then along right field boundary to footbridge and stile at bottom of field.
- Continue ahead to further stile and climb towards buildings. Just before buildings, go left over stile and after 70 yards go right over further stile. Go diagonally right to stile and follow path to emerge on Stubby Lane in Draycott-in-the-Clay.
- Go left, passing 'tin tabernacle', and cross A515 on to Pipehay Lane. Go right on Greaves Lane and after 200 yards go left over stile. Go diagonally right downhill to stile and footbridge. Go left and rise up bank to stile at end of hedge. Go diagonally right rising through field to stile and continue on same line aiming for church spire.
- At end of long field go left over stile and climb 50 yards to further stile on right. Go ahead on rising path to left of woodland to stile. Go right to further stile, then go left to pass St Werburgh's church in Hanbury.

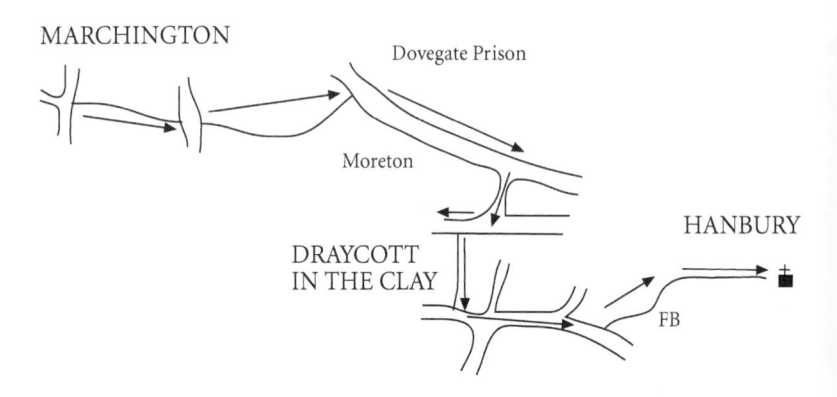

DRAYCOTT-IN-THE-CLAY

The most notable thing about the tiny settlement of Draycott-in-the-Clay is the church of St Augustine. It is an example of a 'tin tabernacle' church, such as were thrown up at a time when people were clamouring for religion but could not afford the standard big-stone model. It is a lovely little black and white building, much loved by the villagers.

Draycott-in-the-Clay also boasts a pub, The Swan, and the Klondyke Mill Steam Preservation Centre, where steam rallies are held to attract steam nuts from all round. The village also has an annual agricultural show every September. So it's not as tiny as it looks.

HANBURY

The large church of St Werburgh, high on a hill in the village of Hanbury, takes its name from the Saxon Princess Werburgh who founded a nunnery in 680 and was buried here in 703. The early church became a place of pilgrimage but, when threatened with Viking attacks, her relics were transferred to Chester in 875. The modern church was extensively rebuilt in the 14th century and then again in the 19th century.

There are a number of fascinating tombs and memorials inside the lovely old church, including that of Sir John de Hanbury, who is believed to have died in 1303. The busts of Mrs Katherine Agard and her daughter Ann in their Puritan hats and ruffs sternly overlook the pulpit as if to warn any modern vicars to restrain themselves from any excessive behaviour, such as wearing sandals or playing the guitar.

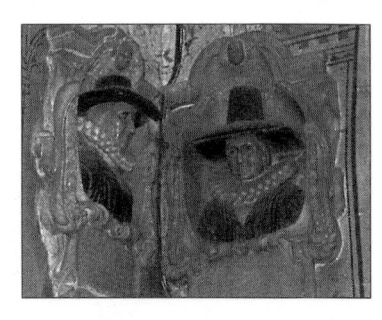

Hanbury – Tutbury (3 miles)

- Follow Church Lane past St Werburgh's, bending right to pass Post Office. At T-junction go left on Martins Lane and then left again on Hanbury Hill. Just before Cock Inn & Fauld Explosion sign go right through gate on to footpath. Follow through three further gates on to narrow fenced path to gate.
- Go diagonally left to gate in bottom corner of field. Continue straight ahead to further gate into woodland. Go immediately right through gate and follow fence around Fauld Explosion site *(N.B. Danger – Unexploded Bombs)* to memorial.
- Go through gate and after 200 yards follow footpath sign on right to gate. Cross field to further gate and continue to squeeze stile. Go left rising to double stile across farm track. Continue ahead descending to plank bridge and stile.
- Go right following right field boundary round to double stile. Follow right field boundary over two more double stiles and then over squeeze stile, following left field boundary to Castle Hayes Park Farm. Take track past farm buildings and, where track bends right, follow footpath sign across two fields to rejoin track *(N.B. Tutbury Castle visible ahead)*.
- After 50 yards go through gateway on to narrow path to stile, then follow right field boundary over two squeeze stiles to end of field. Go right over squeeze stile and after 20 yards left over stile.
- Follow right field boundary over three squeeze stiles and bend left at bottom of field. Continue downhill to reach road. Go straight across on to path beside house, then go diagonally right up through gate and then towards Tutbury Castle, eventually emerging over stile on to road.
- Go left and follow Castle Street down to reach junction with High Street. Go left for Old Dog & Partridge (01283-813030).

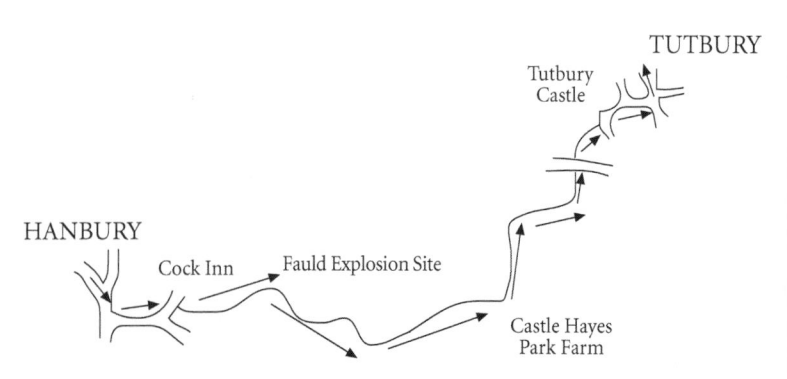

FAULD EXPLOSION

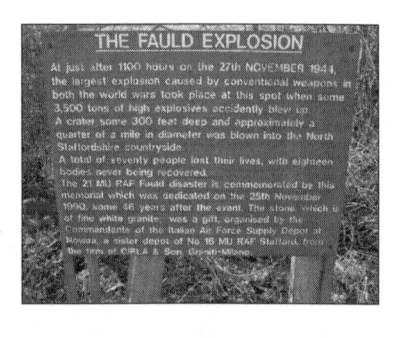

On 27th November 1944 Hanbury witnessed its worst ever tragedy. The RAF had commandeered an old gypsum mine just outside the village in which to build an underground storage depot for 4000 tons of explosives. Somehow there was a massive explosion of all these bombs, throwing up a huge mushroom cloud with huge mounds of earth and trees being thrown into the air. When everything cleared some days later what was left was a huge crater, half a mile in width and one hundred feet in depth. All RAF personnel and Italian prisoners-of-war working underground, seventy-eight in total, were killed and there was extensive damage to all the buildings in the area, including the Cock Inn which tells the story of the Fauld Explosion on its walls.

TUTBURY

Tutbury is a very old village, the remains of its castle on a hill looking over the River Dove built on the site of what was an Anglo-Saxon fort. Tutbury Castle was first built shortly after 1066 but was much extended in later centuries. Its most famous residents were John of Gaunt, who spent much time here in the 14th century and introduced bull-running to the town (which lasted until 1778), and Mary Queen of Scots, who was imprisoned here three times by Elizabeth I in the 16th century. The castle was demolished on the orders of Oliver Cromwell.

The village itself is a charming place with its broad High Street containing a number of Georgian buildings. The 14th century Old Dog & Partridge has a high reputation for its food and serves a range of Real Ales, including Adnam's, Marston's and Abbot Ale. It is an appropriate place to break your journey before the last stage of the walk to Burton-upon-Trent.

Tutbury – Burton-upon-Trent (5 miles)

- Turn right outside Old Dog & Partridge and proceed along High Street. Turn right on Cornmill Lane and follow out of village. Shortly after passing Hoblands Farm, go left over stile on to lower path, initially beside stream.
- Near end of field climb up steps on right to stile then follow left field boundary. Continue through long field to stile. Follow right field boundary for 30 yards then go through gap in hedge on to left field boundary. Continue on clear footpath over four stiles to reach road.
- Go left 100 yards then right over stile. Go diagonally right towards Dove Lea, emerging via alleyway on to Marston Road. Go left up to T-junction, then left again on Church Road to pass St Mary's church and the Spread Eagle pub in Rolleston-on-Dove.
- Continue ahead on Station Road. Take second right, Chapel Lane, and follow as it bends to become Beacon Road. After 100 yards on Beacon Road go left through gate on footpath signposted 'Craythorne Road'. Continue ahead through gate and on to footpath signposted 'Walton Road' into car park.
- In car park go left over stile. Go diagonally right across playing fields to stile in top-corner of field. Continue on path behind houses, then crossing field to steps down to Jinny Trail. Go right and follow, eventually reaching road in Stretton.
- Cross road and continue on footpath. At end of track cross road and continue on same line behind houses to join road passing under A38. On reaching Trent & Mersey Canal, go right on towpath signposted Lichfield. Follow through Horninglow Basin and Dallow Lock *(N.B. fabulous murals)* to reach footbridge.
- Go up to path and turn left to reach road. Go straight across on Casey Lane and follow to reach centre of Burton-upon-Trent.

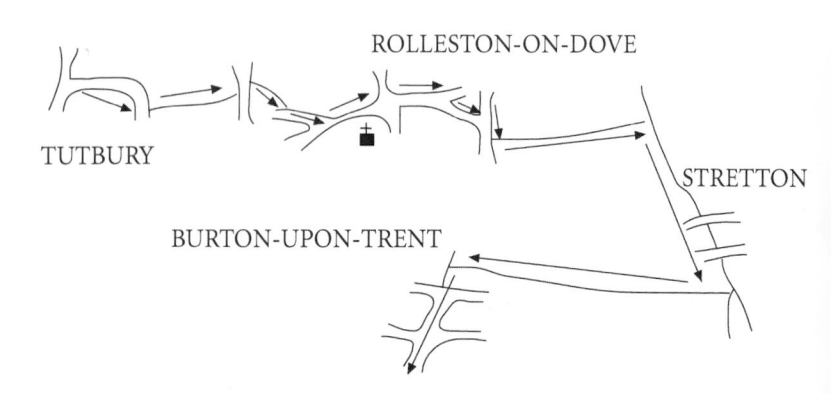

ROLLESTON-ON-DOVE

Rolleston-on-Dove is first mentioned in King Edmund's charter of AD 942 as Rodulfestan. For over a thousand years it has been a small agricultural settlement along the River Dove. Rolleston Hall, now demolished, was for many decades the home of the Mosley family (including the infamous fascist Oswald Mosley), whose heraldic arms incorporated an eagle in flight; hence the name of the village pub, the Spread Eagle.

The North Staffordshire railway arrived in 1848 bringing access to the brewery trade of Burton-upon-Trent, although the station didn't open until 1894. Note, this station is one mile from the village centre, placed there on the orders of Sir Tonman Mosley, Chairman of the Railway Company, who didn't want to be disturbed in Rolleston Hall.

St Mary's church in the centre of the village is basically 13th century Norman from the time of Henry II, though there had been a church on that site for at least 300 years earlier. The church has a number of monuments to prominent citizens of the village, most notably an array of Mosleys, and there is an Anglo-Saxon crosshead just outside the main building.

JINNY NATURE TRAIL

The 'Tutbury Jinny' was the name given to the little train that served the country between Tutbury and Burton-upon-Trent, a distance of about five miles, with intermediate stations at Rolleston on Dove, Clay Mills, Stretton and Horninglow. It ran for over a century, beginning in 1848 and finally closing in 1960.

The train, usually of three coaches, was propelled by a push-pull engine and did several journeys a day, becoming a much-loved institution until its closure. Its last sentimental journey was from Burton-upon-Trent in June 1960, when a train packed with rail enthusiasts was sent on their journey to the strains of a bugler playing 'The Last Post'.

The Jinny Nature trail follows the track of the former railway, its embankments attracting a wide variety of birds and butterflies. The Rolleston section of the Jinny Trail is used for a national butterfly mapping scheme.

BURTON-UPON-TRENT PIX

National Brewery Centre

Burton Bridge Brewery

St Peter

Bass House

Stapenhill Ferry Bridge

Burton Cooper

BURTON-UPON-TRENT STORY

Say for what were hop-yards meant,
Or why was Burton built on Trent?

A.E. Housman

Burton-upon-Trent is renowned throughout the world as the centre of brewing in the United Kingdom, the trade being first developed by the monks of Burton Abbey. The town is, however, Anglo-Saxon, and the first church here was built in the 7th century by the Irish St Modwen. Burton Abbey was also a Saxon settlement, being built by Earl Wulfric in 1003 for the Benedictine order of monks and becoming the largest and richest monastery in Staffordshire. As well as brewing, the monks also developed the wool trade.

After the Dissolution of the Monasteries in 1540, local innkeepers, perhaps recruiting retired monks, started to make their own beer and by the beginning of the 17th century these beers were being sold as far afield as London. Improvements in the navigability of the River Trent in the 18th century opened up the route to the east coast, from where opportunities for trade with the Baltic countries and with Russia opened up – Catherine the Great is said to have been 'immoderately fond' of a pint of Burton beer.

In 1777 the opening of the Trent & Mersey Canal gave access to east and west. In the same year William Bass opened his brewery and the coming of the railways in 1839 gave a further boost to trade, allowing the Burton brewers to export their products. The infamous India Pale Ale became the drink of choice in the ex-pat community. Bass expanded by buying out other Midlands smaller breweries but the same thing has happened to Bass itself, as it has become part of the international American-based conglomerate Coors. A legend has died.

The secret of Burton beer lies in the hard water pumped to the surface from underground springs. The rocks surrounding these springs contain gypsum and the water dissolves out of these, absorbing magnesium and calcium sulphates, giving the water its special quality. In the past brewers from elsewhere in England have sunk wells in Burton-upon-Trent and transported water from them to their own breweries. The large vats needed to produce and store beer, together with the large buildings necessary for storing and drying grain, still dominate the skyline of the town. The recently-opened National Brewery Centre, situated in what used to be the Bass Museum, pays fitting tribute to the history of beer and brewing in Burton-upon-Trent.

BURTON-UPON-TRENT CELEBRITIES

Edward Wightman (1566-1612)
Edward Wightman was born and died in Burton-upon-Trent, the last person to be burned at the stake for heresy. He ran a mercer's business in the town but was also a minister in the Baptist church, in which position he began preaching extreme religious views about the mortality of the soul. His big mistake was when, awaiting trial for heresy, he sent James I a copy of his religious tract, thus bringing his parochial case into more public view. The king ordered his execution and he was burned to ashes in front of the crowd.

William Bass (1717-1787)
William Bass was the founder of Bass Brewery, whose beers helped to make Burton-upon-Trent synonymous with excellent beer throughout the 19th and 20th centuries. Originally a carrier of beer, Bass started his own brewery in 1777 to exploit the growing fame of Burton beers. In 1784 he started exporting beer directly to Russia and Bass Pale Ale was exported all over the British Empire. Bass Brewers was taken over by the American Coors in 2000 but Bass Pale Ale is still brewed by Marston's Brewery in Burton-upon-Trent.

William Coltman (1891-1974)
William Coltman was the most decorated other rank of the First World War, as a stretcher-bearer. He was a twenty-six year old Lance Corporal serving in France in the North Staffordshire Regiment. On several occasions Coltman under heavy fire rescued several of his wounded colleagues and brought them back to safety. For these acts of bravery he was awarded successively the Military Medal, the Distinguished Service Medal and Bar, and finally the Victoria Cross 'for most conspicuous bravery, initiative and devotion to duty'.

Phil Seamen (1926-1972)
Some people claim that Phil Seamen was Europe's greatest ever jazz drummer. Growing up in the big band era, Seamen got his first professional engagement with Nat Gonella's band in 1944. He went on to play with all the well-known British bands, including those of Jack Parnell, Stan Tracey, Ronnie Scott and Tubby Hayes. He also taught Ginger Baker, later to be Cream's drummer. Sadly his talent was hounded by alcoholism and heroin addiction and on his death the pathologist stated that the level of barbiturates in him technically meant that he was dead long before he actually died.

BURTON-UPON-TRENT CAKES

CAFÉ B, High Street
Very popular café in centre of town offering wide range of tasty cakes, snacks, coffees and teas and hot chocolate. Friendly and helpful staff and comfy furniture but can be very busy at certain times.

MOCHA, New Street
Modern café with traditional seating and leather sofas. Good range of cakes and snacks offered, as well as coffees, teas and hot chocolate. Relaxed and friendly place.

BURTON-UPON-TRENT ALE

BURTON BRIDGE INN, Bridge Street
17th century home of Burton Bridge Brewery, so has up to seven of own Real Ales on tap regularly. Food served at lunchtime only. Has skittle alley upstairs and two rooms downstairs. CAMRA recommended.

COOPERS TAVERN, Cross Street
Originally the home of Bass Brewery but now privately-owned free house with barrel tables and bench seats in tap room. Serves Bass, Tower Thomas Salt and Hop Back Summer Lightning. CAMRA recommended.

DERBY INN, Derby Road
Brick-built local pub in northern end of town, harking back to 1950s with old memorabilia and locally-produced vegetables, fruit and produce on sale at bar. Serves Marston's, Jennings and Banks's. CAMRA recommended.

DEVONSHIRE ARMS, Station Street
19th century pub in listed building with unusual arched ceilings and fountain in patio. Serves Burton Bridge Real Ales and food on Fridays and Saturdays. CAMRA recommended.

WETMORE WHISTLE, Wetmore Road
Refurbished by Tynemill and only two rooms but attractive with wooden floors, part-tiled walls. Serves Bass, Marston's, Bateman's, Castle Rock and other Real Ales. Also offers food. CAMRA recommended.

BURTON-UPON-TRENT ACCOMMODATION

Delter Hotel, 5 Derby Road, Burton-upon-Trent, DE14 1RU
(Tel: 01283-535115)

Grail Court Hotel, Station Street, Burton-upon-Trent, DE14 1BN
(Tel: 01283-741155)

Premier Travel Inn, Ashby Road East, Burton-upon-Trent, DE15 0PU
(Tel: 01283-219562)

Redmoor House, 6 Redmoor Close, Winshill, Burton upon Trent, DE15 0HZ (Tel: 01283-531977)

Three Queens Hotel, Bridge Street, Burton-upon-Trent, DE14 1SY
(Tel:01283-523800)

Wendy's B&B, 22 Yarrow Close, Brizlincote Valley, Burton-upon-Trent, DE15 9JT (Tel: 07929-075298)

BURTON-UPON-TRENT SERVICES

Post Office: in Asda Supermarket, Octagon Centre

Banks with ATM: Barclays, HSBC, Lloyds and NatWest, all in centre of town

Tourist Information Centre: Market Place (01283-508111)

Transport connections: mainline railway station

USEFUL INFORMATION

Tourist/Visitor Information Centres

Lichfield, Lichfield Garrick, Castle Dyke, Lichfield, WS13 6HR
(Tel: 01543-412112)

Burton-upon-Trent, Market Place, High Street, Burton-upon-Trent, DE14 1AH (Tel: 01283-508000)

Cannock (for Cannock Chase), The Valley Heritage Centre, Valley Road, Hednesford, WS12 5TD (Tel: 01543-877666)

Stafford (for Penkridge, Eccleshall & Stone), Eastgate Street, Stafford, ST16 2LT (Tel: 01785-619619)

Leek (for Uttoxeter), 1 Market Place, Leek ST13 5HH
(Tel: 01538-483741)

Cheadle, Councils Connect, 15a/17 High Street, Cheadle, ST10 1AA
(Tel: 01538-483860)

Other Contacts

National Rail Enquiries (Tel: 08457-484950)

West Midlands Traveline (Tel: 0871-200-2233)

Useful Websites

www.visitlichfield.co.uk

www.visitstafford.co.uk

www.enjoystaffordshire.co.uk

www.staffsmoorlands.gov.uk

www.eaststaffsbc.gov.uk

www.nationalbrewerycentre.co.uk

SUGGESTED READING

Anon (1996), *The Staffordshire Way*, Staffordshire County Council

Clayton, Howard (1992), *Cathedral City: a Look at Victorian Lichfield*, Abbotsford

Fisher, Michael (1999) *Alton Towers: A Gothic Wonderland*, Michael Fisher

Gibson, Alan (2003), *A History of Rocester*, Churnet Valley Books

Johnson, Samuel (2006), *A Dictionary of the English Language: An Anthology*, Penguin

King-Hele, Desmond, *Erasmus Darwin: A Life of Unequalled Achievement*, Giles de la Mare

Pevsner, Nikolaus (1974), *The Buildings of England: Staffordshire*, Penguin

Protz, Roger (ed.), *Good Beer Guide 2012*, CAMRA Books

Raven, Michael (1988), *Staffordshire and the Black Country*, Michael Raven

Redfern, Francis (2010), *History of the Town of Uttoxeter*, Unknown

Roberts, John (2000), *The Heart of England Way*, Walkways

Staffordshire Federation of Women's Institutes (1998), *The Staffordshire Village Book*, Countryside Books

Stone, Richard (2004), *Burton upon Trent: a History*, Phillimore & Co

Stone, Richard (2007), *The Collieries and Coalminers of Staffordshire*, Phillimore & Co

Tames, Richard (2001), *Josiah Wedgwood: An Illustrated Life*, Shire Publications

Wheat, Rose (2009), *Penkridge in the Late Seventeenth Century*, Penkridge Civic Society

Wilkes, Robert Charles (1985), *The Story of Penkridge*, Penkridge Parish Council

DISTANCE CHECKLIST

SECTION 1	DAILY MILES	TOTAL MILES
BURTON-UPON-TRENT	-	-
Dunstall	4.5	4.5
Alrewas	8.5	8.5
Fradley Junction	10.5	10.5
LICHFIELD	13.5	13.5

SECTION 2	DAILY MILES	TOTAL MILES
LICHFIELD	-	13.5
Cresswell Green	3	16.5
Castle Ring	6	19.5
Chase Visitor Centre	9.5	23
Bednall	13.5	27
PENKRIDGE	16.5	30

SECTION 3	DAILY MILES	TOTAL MILES
PENKRIDGE	-	30
Church Eaton	6	36
Gnosall	9	39
Ellenhall	13.5	43.5
ECCLESHALL	15.5	45.5

SECTION 4	DAILY MILES	TOTAL MILES
ECCLESHALL	-	45.5
Millmeece	3	48.5
Swynnerton	5	50.5
Trent & Mersey Canal	9	54.5
Barlaston	11	56.5
STONE	14	59.5

SECTION 5	DAILY MILES	TOTAL MILES
STONE	-	59.5
Hilderstone	3	62.5
Moddershall	5	64.5
Saverley Green	8	67.5
CHEADLE	13.5	73

SECTION 6	DAILY MILES	TOTAL MILES
CHEADLE	-	73
Hawksmoor	2.5	75.5
Alton	5.5	78.5
Denstone	8	81
Rocester	10	83
UTTOXETER	14	87

SECTION 7	DAILY MILES	TOTAL MILES
UTTOXETER	-	87
Marchington	3	90
Hanbury	6	93
Tutbury	9	96
BURTON-UPON TRENT	14	101